Splish Splash

Splish Splash

My Life in and Out of the Water

Tom De Long with Sharon Hastings

© 2017 Tom De Long with Sharon Hastings
All rights reserved.
ISBN-13: 9781539982418
ISBN-10: 1539982416

Contents

	Prologue	vii
One	Beginnings	1
Two	Relatives	4
Three	Las Vegas	10
Four	Arkansas	14
Five	Phoenix	20
Six	Long Beach	28
Seven	Diving	31
Eight	Football	35
Nine	University of Denver	39
Ten	Love and Marriage	43
Eleven	Clown Diving	47
Twelve	Lifeguarding	49
Thirteen	Coaching	55
Fourteen	The Early Years at Foothill	58
Fifteen	Coaching Strategies	61
Sixteen	Foothill Girls' Swimming	65
Seventeen	Foothill Families	67
Eighteen	Water Polo	73
Nineteen	Olympians	76
Twenty	The Results of Foothill Olympic Success	78
Twenty One	Teaching Stories	80
Twenty Two	Coaching Colleagues	83
Twenty Three	The Tom De Long Family	93
Twenty Four	Extended Family	96
Twenty Five	The Next Generation	98
Twenty Six	Grandchildren	102
Twenty Seven	Woodworking	106
Twenty Eight	Sailing	108

Twenty Nine	The Transpac	112
Thirty	Philosophy	118
	Epilogue	123
	Tributes	129
	Index	151
	Author Biography	155
	Appendix A	157
	Appendix B	159

Prologue

Tom De Long woke to rain one spring morning in Southern California in 1965. Despite the inclement weather, he was on top of the world. With a freshly minted teaching certificate in hand, he was in high demand in a state awash with high school baby boomers. He already had two coaching job offers in his hip pocket—one was to take over the fabled swimming program at Newport Harbor High School.

But this day, Tom was driving from his newly purchased home in Costa Mesa to a new high school nestled in orange groves near Tustin. He kissed his lovely wife, Clara—pregnant with their first child—hopped into his vintage Austin-Healey Sprite, and began the thirteen-mile drive to Foothill High School (FHS). Tom first heard of Foothill when he was finishing up his teaching certificate studies at Long Beach State College. He was intrigued. Here was a brand-spanking-new school situated in an emerging, affluent suburb of Orange County. For an ambitious new coach with a storied aquatic pedigree, Foothill might just provide him with the opportunity to build a swimming program rather than to continue one.

In 1965, there was no Newport Freeway—or the 55, as it is now called. Tom took the three-lane Newport Highway after leaving the neighborhood streets of Costa Mesa. With no stop signs until Tustin, he drove at a good clip, passing acres of bean fields followed by acres and acres of ripening strawberries. Off to his right were the huge blimp barns at El Toro Marine Base. Once in the sleepy town of Tustin, he slowed his car as he passed tidy little homes built in the 1920s and 1930s and then drove the remaining mile and a half to Foothill. All told, the trip from Costa Mesa took less than twenty minutes.

Beyond an innate confidence in himself and a belief in the winning traditions he had experienced and the coaches he had learned from at Long Beach Poly High School, Long Beach City College, and the University of Denver, Coach De Long had no knowledge that he would one day lead Foothill teams to multiple CIF (California Interscholastic Federation) championships and to coach four athletes to Olympic glory. That spring day in 1965, he was just a twenty-seven-year-old diver and Long Beach lifeguard chasing down a hunch.

Tom drove into the Foothill parking lot off Dodge Avenue. When he stepped from his car, he filled his lungs with damp air slightly scented with the perfume of orange blossoms and the more acrid smell of eucalyptus trees. Aside from a few homes across the street, the school was surrounded by orange groves and sheltered by eucalyptus windbreaks. If you looked closely, you could see the squat shapes of smudge pots in and among the trees—with an occasional propeller to stir the air on near-freezing nights.

Tom De Long with Sharon Hastings

His blond hair shining even on a dark day, Tom walked onto campus. He now smelled the scents of new construction. Directly ahead of him, workers were pouring the concrete forms that would eventually be the flanged roof of the snack bar and school cafeteria. Farther in the distance, other workers were pouring concrete into huge walls that would soon be raised to form the new Foothill High School gymnasium. An accomplished builder himself, Tom marveled at the new building techniques and technologies he was seeing. The sights, sounds, and smells of "new" encouraged Tom that his hunch about Foothill might be right.

Foothill Athletic Director Bob Osborne met Tom in the big lecture hall situated in the main wing of the school. The two men had an instant connection. One by one, Tom met the other Foothill coaches. They all shared an excitement and energy about what they could potentially build at the brand-new high school. Later in the day, Tom met with Tustin High School District Athletic Director Bud Goddell, who was also enthusiastic and impressive. It was an exciting and eye-opening day for the young coach. Although he had a verbal offer in hand to coach the most successful high school swim program in Southern California, Tom left Foothill that day thinking his future may well lie with a different school. Now he was going to make a bet that would define his life. Here, in Coach's own words, are some of the thoughts and feelings he was experiencing.

When I took the job at Foothill, I,d been offered a job at Newport Harbor High School. We were to sit down on a Saturday morning to finalize the deal. I met with Bob Osborne at Foothill during that week—a Tuesday or Wednesday—and he all but offered me the Foothill job based on our meeting. I came home and told Clara about this little school that was tucked away in a bunch of orange groves in Tustin. Bob and I had walked out between the girls' and boys' locker rooms that had just been built—the gym was under construction. Bob showed me the weed-covered lot where the swimming pool was going to be. I have always been a nut for where you put a swimming pool and its relationship to the afternoon sun. The pool was to be on the west side of the gym. The first thought that went through my mind was, "This is cool; we won't have a late-afternoon shadow across the pool." As a diver, I knew that the best-placed diving boards faced north—which put the sun to the divers' backs. These are crazy things that were going through my mind! In my own pool at home, I placed the deep end where the diving board would put your back to the sun.

I came home after the meeting and told Clara, "I don't think I am going to take the job at Newport Harbor. I think I'll take the job at Foothill. I'll get to start my own program from scratch; I won't be following in Jack Fullerton and Al Irwin's footsteps." Plus, the Newport Harbor pools were awful at that time. There was a small diving pool where they played water polo. Then, in the racing pool, the lanes were all in shallow water. Although the facilities were later revamped, no one mentioned those plans to me when we were interviewing.

So, I went back to Foothill and met with Bob Osborne again. After that second meeting, I came home and told Clara that I was definitely going to turn down the job at Newport Harbor. In those days, the hiring process included a breakfast meeting with the district school superintendent, the athletic director, and the school principal. I was scheduled to have breakfast on Saturday morning with the superintendent of the Newport School District, the principal at Newport Harbor, and the athletic director. On Thursday, I called and told them that I had accepted another job. I made the decision, then drove back up to Foothill, and told them that I wanted the job. Just like that, that's how I ended up at Foothill.

However, the actual road to Foothill High School was for Tom De Long far lengthier, more convoluted, and more interesting than the one he drove that spring morning in 1965.

One

Beginnings

Andre Pierre De Long was born in Hawthorne, Nevada, on October 2, 1937. He was a scrawny little guy at twenty-two inches long and a weight of five pounds even. At birth, he looked more like a basketball player than the champion diver he was to become. His appearance was so odd that his uncle Bud asked Coach's mother if she really thought she was going to raise "it."

Coach's days as Andy De Long did not last. The family quickly decided that the name Andre Pierre did not fit their active, little infant. Tom's dad was the one who decided on the name that stuck: Thomas Edward De Long.

Little Tom De Long had an older brother, Paul Joseph, who was six years older than he. His sister, Marjorie Lee, was five years older. Tom was a happy, towheaded bundle of energy who charmed his family with his little round face and chubby cheeks. Years later, his Gerber baby looks would earn him a Cutest Baby Teacher award at Foothill High School.

> A story I was told about myself as a baby was that I'd finish my bottle and flip it out of the crib—until I'd broken all the baby bottles they had. My mom told me they ended up putting a nipple onto a ketchup bottle and gave me my milk in that. The ketchup bottle was thick, so when I'd throw it out—there wasn't carpeting—it wouldn't break. Mom would hear it hit the floor, and she'd know that I was finished with my bottle. That ketchup bottle was indestructible—no more broken glass or hungry baby!

Tom's first memories are as a small boy living in San Bernardino, California. San Bernardino was a hot, dusty town in those days. No one had air conditioning, and kids made their own fun. The De Longs lived near an icehouse where locally grown produce was stored. Brothers Paul and Tom hung out near the building on hot days and would often be rewarded when a watermelon hit the ground and the workmen would give them the shattered fruit. The boys had another reason, too.

> In those days, most people kept their food cold at home in iceboxes. The iceman would deliver the ice to you. I can remember a guy at the icehouse chipping giant blocks of ice. He had a huge piece of leather that fit over his shoulder. He'd hoist huge fifty or seventy-five-pound blocks of ice, throw them up on his shoulder, and then carry them. In the summer, my brother

and I'd just sit and watch him. He was impressive. But we'd always grab a piece of newspaper before we went. He'd throw us the chips that flew when his pick hit the ice; some were pretty fair sized. Trouble was, they were too cold to hold on to, so we'd wrap them in the newspaper. Then we'd just suck on that ice. It was a nice way to stay cool in the summer.

Tom and his older brother were always making up fun for themselves. Good-natured Paul let Tom tag along with him and his friends—even though Tom was so much younger.

As a kid, I loved climbing trees. I'd climb any tree that I could get a hold of. We lived right next to a Goodwill facility. After business hours, there was a place where trucks could make after-hours deliveries. The goods were taken from the trucks and then slid down wooden slides to sorting tables where they would be processed the following morning. Those slides were unbelievably slippery. Well, my brother and I and some of his friends would climb up a tree and step over onto the top of the Goodwill fence. Then we'd slide down those slides, landing in big containers of clothing. We'd get out, climb up to the top, and slide down again and again. It was a pretty good distance, and we got going fast. That's a fun early memory of mine.

Times were different then. World War II was on, and recovery from the Great Depression was still under way. Pleasures were pretty simple but no less fondly remembered.

We were—I just have to say—we were poor. I can remember early on—during the war—there was a lot of rationing. Butter was hard to come by. The margarine, which was almost white, would come with packets of dye that looked like the little packets of parmesan cheese you sometimes get at pizza places—only brighter orange. My mom would allow me—if I really scrubbed my hands—to mix the colorant into the margarine by hand. I used to love to do that. You'd mix the powder in and then shape the margarine into a ball on a butter dish.

Later, my big treat was sneaking in the house—and kind of like pickup sticks—trying to pick a knife out of the utensil drawer without making any noise. Then I would spread margarine on a piece of bread and sprinkle sugar on it. That was "sneak a treat" for me. I'm not sure how many times I was successful in doing that; I remember I got caught a bunch of times.

I just loved hot dogs when I was a kid—cold hot dogs. I was babysat by Mr. and Mrs. Blanding, a couple who owned a little grocery store. They had a small meat case, and after I got up from my nap, I got to go open the meat case and take out a cold hot dog. I used to love that. It's a memory that really sticks in my mind.

A couple of Coach's childhood memories are much less the stuff of Norman Rockwell. Hard times in the country affected the De Long family.

My index finger on my right hand doesn't bend past the middle knuckle. One day, I was threatening my sister because she wouldn't let me go to the store with her. I had a butcher knife, and I was holding it by the blade. My brother apparently came up behind me and took the knife away from me. You can imagine what happened. It cut all four of my fingers, but most seriously, it cut the tendon in my index finger. I can remember sitting in the sink with blood all over everything—then they got me to a hospital. At that time, all the medical specialists were gone to World War II. So, the doctor at the hospital was unable to reconnect the tendon. Even in those days, if a specialist had been available, it would have been a pretty easy repair job. So, I lost some function in that hand. Still, even though this was my right hand, and I'm right-handed, I have had no problems. Kids adapt. But it turns out my strongest memory of that day is getting an all-day sucker—for bravery. I can't remember now if I ever got in trouble for threatening Marjorie!

A very significant memory I have from those early days happened when I was about four. My father took my brother, sister, and me to the Orange Show Fairgrounds in San Bernardino. In my mind, I can still see this long string of tickets that my brother was carrying. We rode the merry-go-round for hours using all those tickets. But when we were finished, my dad was gone. Adios.

I can remember we were taken home in a police car. I don't remember what was said by the police or by my mother. That was the last time I remember seeing my dad. It was a horrible day, though I really can't remember much about it. I think it must have been infinitely more traumatic for my brother and sister because they were older—old enough for it to have burned a strong memory. There might have been trouble in the marriage, but I'm not sure. Dad was in the military and this was during the war.

Two

Relatives

Two strong women, his mother, Evelyn Crews De Long Mullikin, and his grandmother, Pearl Lee Mullikin Gilbert, framed Coach De Long's early childhood.

Evelyn Cruz De Long Mullikin, Coach's mom, was a five foot two dynamo of a woman—all smiles and personality. "Five foot two, eyes of blue—that was Mom," says Coach.

> My mom was a bit stocky, and she seemed to have a chronic back problem. She wore a corset to help. But her back never seemed to stop her or get her down. She was very outgoing, and everybody in the neighborhood loved her.
>
> Even though her name was really Evelyn, she got the nickname Peggy. Before she was married, she'd worked in a peach-packing plant in Kansas. Somebody there called her Peaches Peggy. The "Peaches" eventually got dropped, but from then on, she was known as Peggy by everybody.

Peggy was an accomplished seamstress and spent much of her work life sewing to make money for the family. When the family moved to Long Beach, she worked for years at the blue jeans factory there. She also sewed her own clothes and those of her children. Later, she sewed for her daughter's two daughters. Of course, Peggy was a prime mover in the motels the family ran and in their Arkansas chicken business.

> What I learned from my mom is the everyday value of hard work—just sticking to it every day. She was dedicated to her three kids. Family was very important to her—every day of her life. When my sister, Marjorie, lived near her in Lakewood, she would come over to Mom's house, and the kids would get dressed for school over there. She and Mom would have coffee. Mom sewed all their dresses. She was a woman who worked very hard all her life.

Coach's mom died in 1977 at the age of sixty-three. Even in her last months, she was still delighting her family by doing the Charleston. But she had been an avid cigarette smoker all her life, and she succumbed to complications from lung disease. Her grandkids, Ty and Courtnee De Long, were nine and eleven years old. They have wonderful memories of their grandmother. "She just died way, way too soon," says Coach. "Smoking can be so hard for families."

The other strong woman in Coach's childhood was his maternal grandmother, Grandma Pearl, who lived with the family through much of Coach's childhood. In fact, her son-in-law, Rufus Mullikin, eventually married Coach's mother after Peggy's divorce from Tom's real dad. Peggy and Rufus met when Rufus came to visit Grandma Pearl.

Pearl was a formidable woman in all ways. She dreamed big dreams, and her leadership led her daughter, Peggy, and her family on many life adventures during Coach's childhood. Pearl got the family into the motel business. Later, she was the one who took them across the country to her childhood home in Arkansas, where the family took up chicken farming.

> My grandmother was nurturing, as I remember. Of course, my relationship with her as a young adult was quite different than it was when I was seven, eight, nine, ten years old. I remember she had hair so long that it extended below her bottom. It was gray. She'd comb that hair, braid it, and then wrap it around into a huge bun at the nape of her neck. It was a hairstyle from the forties, and she kept that same hairstyle her entire life. It was very nice-looking. Dressing always took her a long while. By the time she got her corset on and did her hair, the morning was near half over! She never was a grandmother to wear black lace-up shoes, but I do remember she always wore black shoes with very low heels. In most ways, she was a very old-fashioned grandma.

Grandma Pearl was a disciplinarian with a heart of gold. Coach has many memories of the ways she made him toe the line. He was a likable but challenging youngster.

> An early memory I have is that my grandmother would give us—I think it was ten cents each day—to buy milk at school. My cousins and I decided we wanted boxing gloves. Each day, we would forgo our milk, and we'd put our money in an old bottle we hid under the house. One day, my grandmother caught one of my cousins crawling toward the bottle. By then, we'd been saving for a long time. Well, my grandmother found that jar of money and confiscated it. We were just devastated. But the neat end to the story is that my grandmother gave us a set of boxing gloves for Christmas.
>
> My grandmother did a lot of sewing and mending. She wore a metal thimble on her left middle finger, and she always seemed to me to have the world's longest arms. She could zap you in the back of the head three or four times with that thimble before you could get away. That's what she always did to my cousins and me when we misbehaved. And I remember how that used to just sting! We'd rub our heads like crazy. From the number of knots I always had on my head, she zapped me a lot!

Grandma Pearl stayed in Phoenix when the family moved to Long Beach. She married a man named Gilbert after the family left. Pearl died in 1957 after unsuccessful gall bladder surgery. In those days, such a death was not uncommon. Coach remembers her to have been about seventy-five years old. She's buried in Long Beach as Pearl Gilbert.

> I believe 1957 is the right year. I remember that Pat McCormick [diving gold medalist at the 1956 Olympics] had given me two Olympic diving pins from the 1956 Melbourne Olympics—where she was a gold medal winner. To this day, I still wear one of those pins on my favorite sports jacket. But I put the other pin on my grandmother's dress at her funeral. I just wanted it to be buried with her.

Coach does not know a great deal about his birth father, Joseph De Long. After abandoning his family, Joseph returned to the town where he had grown up in Indiana. His family had emigrated there from Holland, and Coach is Dutch on the paternal side of the family.

The man who raised Tom De Long was his mom's second husband, Rufus Mullikin. Peggy and Rufus were actually stepbrother and stepsister, as Peggy's mom, Pearl, was married to Rufus's dad. The couple met in Las Vegas during the time the De Long family was managing a hotel there. One night, a six foot four, thin sailor came up to the motel front desk. He had an MP [military police] patch around his arm. He was stationed in San Diego but had been sent to Las Vegas to collect some sailors who'd gone AWOL while gambling.

> My stepdad came from Twin Falls, Idaho. He had dark hair, dark eyes—he seemed a typical tall, thin guy. But he had a huge Japanese fan tattooed on his back; I was so fascinated by that. The tattoo was about the size of a big man's head. It had, as I remember, some Geisha girls on it. In World War II, Rufus was stationed on a seagoing tug stationed in Hawaii. I think he got the tattoo while he was in Hawaii.

Peggy and Rufus began dating and eventually married. As Coach remembers, it must have been a quick romance. It wasn't long after they married that the family picked up and moved to Arkansas. Still, there was time for the new family to move into a little house off New York Avenue in Las Vegas. Coach had some fine adventures there that will be described later.

> My stepdad taught me something that has stayed with me all my life. He was the one to make me understand the value of self-reliance. We didn't get along in many regards. I sometimes thought he was jealous of the love my mom had for me. By the time she and he married, my brother and sister were already in high school. I was still in the nest.
>
> But he used to tell me, "The best helping hand you'll ever find in life is found at the end of your own arm." I've never forgotten that.

Rufus finished out his career on the production line at the Ford Motor plant in Pico Rivera, California. The family and he drifted apart after Peggy's death, and they became estranged when Rufus took a new wife who didn't fit well with Tom's family. Coach regrets that his stepdad was not closer to his grandchildren. In retirement, Rufus became a chauffeur to an older woman who owned several clothing stores in Southern California. Sometimes they would drive by the De Long home and honk but not stop. Later in his life, Rufus would occasionally make a "flyby" visit. Coach recalls, "I could be wrong, but it seems like every time he came to visit us, he would stay twenty minutes and then have to get going." Rufus lived only a few years after the death of Coach's mom.

Splish Splash

Paul Joseph De Long is six years Coach's senior. The two brothers look alike, although Coach describes his brother as the handsome one.

> If I were to show you a picture of him at age twenty-five, you'd say, "That's Marlon Brando"—he was Hollywood handsome as a young man when he first went into the army.

The two boys hung out together as kids, despite their age difference. In fact, Paul once saved Coach's life.

> There were sand and gravel pits near where we lived in San Bernardino. They'd fill with water—and I had a near-drowning experience in one of them. There was a steep gravel incline, and I can remember just sliding—not being able to stop—and going right into the water. My brother was in hot pursuit. I remember having my eyes open and being under water. And then my brother pulled me out of the water. I was probably four or five years old and had zero time in the water. I couldn't swim at all. My brother doesn't remember grabbing me by the hair that day at the rock quarry. But that's one of those things that freezes in your mind forever.
>
> After that experience, my mom decided maybe I should know how to swim. I learned to swim at the Highland Park Pool. It was on Highland Avenue. They call it Baseline now. It's at the foot of the San Bernardino Mountains on the way to the resorts up there. We had to take a bus to get there. I was five years old, and I was taught to swim by my brother and the lifeguards at the pool.

Like Coach, Paul was a risk-taker and a kid hell-bent on fun. Tom idolized his brother.

> Paul was a great big brother to me. He was always looking out for me, and I really looked up to—and admired—him. He was my big brother. He made sure that I got to go places when he and his friends would do things. Maybe sometimes I was too young to do those things—but he always had his eye on me. A couple of times in Las Vegas, I remember instances where Paul and his friends got into trouble, and because I was with them, I was on the verge, but Paul somehow always kept me safe.

When Paul left home, he went into the army and did two tours of duty in Korea. He was in charge of a track-mounted Howitzer cannon. And he saw enough hard combat to develop posttraumatic stress syndrome.

> I can remember a couple of times waking up at night and he was on top of me—just pounding the devil out of me. He had really bad nightmares from his time in Korea.

Paul spent an entire career in the army and ended up as a sergeant first class. His first wife's name was Norma Jean Courtnee. Eventually, that marriage came apart.

After Paul's stint in Japan, he was stationed in France, where he edited the *Stars and Stripes*. He also spent a tour at the Pentagon, where he was involved with army education programs because of his experience editing the newspaper. While Paul was in France, he met and married his second wife, a Frenchwoman named Madeleine. They had two children together, Paul Jr. and Patsy. Paul Jr. now lives in the Anaheim, California, area. Patsy lives in Arlington, Virginia, and her family is very involved with Civil War reenactments.

When Coach's brother, Paul, retired from the army, he worked as a truck driver for a while. Then he went back to California State University, Long Beach, to finish up his degree. He taught geography at Long Beach City College and at Orange Coast College. Several years ago, he moved to Crescent City—near the California/Oregon border. He now lives in Brookings, Oregon.

Marjorie Lee De Long Hoban was Coach's sister. Five years older than Tom, she was old enough to have her own interests and friends, and the two kids were never especially close. Besides, Tom was the baby in the De Long family, and his mom sometimes favored him. Many times, both Paul and Marjorie accused him of being his mom's favorite. Coach speculates he may have occasionally irritated his older sister.

> My sister was good to me later on. She pursued a career in hairdressing. When I was young, I used to bite my fingernails. She told me that if I didn't bite my fingernails for six months, then she'd buy me a bike. I made the six months, and she bought me a bike. This was in Long Beach, and I ended up riding that bike to school every day all through junior high.

Marjorie graduated from high school in Phoenix. She changed her name to Maggie and started cosmetology school when the family lived in Long Beach She cut and/or styled the hair of everyone in the family.

Maggie married Ed Hoban in the early fifties, and they had two daughters, Randi and Jan. Maggie's husband worked for a linen supply company and drove a truck delivering uniforms. Coach's mom, Peggy, loved her two granddaughters. Maggie's family lived just a couple of blocks away from Peggy, Rufus, and Tom.

> Every morning, my mom would make coffee, and my sister would come over with the two girls. They'd still be in their pajamas, and they'd get dressed at Mother's house. My mother did all their laundry and starched and ironed all their dresses. She also made dresses for the girls. Often, my sister would even get dressed there before she went to work.

Maggie died very young, in her early fifties, in a sky-diving accident. It was hard on the family, but they felt comforted knowing that she died doing something she loved.

Joseph "Bud" Cruz was Peggy's brother and Coach's favorite uncle. He and his family were very close to Coach and his family during the years in San Bernardino, Las Vegas, and Arkansas.

> I liked Uncle Bud very much. He used to tease me when I was little. He would get some ketchup on his finger, and then he'd take a table knife and grab me. He'd put the dull side toward my ear—but I wouldn't know that. He'd take that knife and pretend to cut my ear off! Then the ketchup would look like blood on his hands. He'd say, "I'm going to cut your ear off!" It scared the devil out of me until I figured out what he was doing, and then I'd just play along. I'd hold

my ear and say, "Oh no, you cut my ear off!" But of course, he had his own three sons. So, he had many ears to choose from.

Before we moved to Las Vegas, Uncle Bud ran an orange grove in the San Bernardino area. This was when I was about six or seven. A big thrill for me was to go out to the orange grove and play. These orange trees were not trimmed, so they hung all the way to the ground. My cousins and I found places where we'd hide in the trees. One day, we found a hubcap and decided to create a new game. We took the hubcap and rolled it into the street that ran through the orchard. It would roll by passing cars, and the drivers would think it was theirs and stop. Then we'd grab the hubcap and run. Of course, the driver would chase us because he thought we were stealing his hubcap. We'd dodge our way through the orange trees to hide.

The best fun was when the orchard had been recently irrigated; those drivers would be yelling and running and sloshing through mud! They could never find us because we all had our hiding places. The driver would go back to his car—covered in mud—only to find all four hubcaps on the car. We were stinkers, but that was a fun thing we used to do. Eventually, we got caught. Some young guy caught us, marched us to our house, and we all got in trouble.

We did some crazy things. We weren't vicious or anything. But we did find things to occupy our time.

Uncle Bud became a machinist after the failure of the chicken farm in Arkansas. He didn't move to Phoenix with the family. Later, Tom remembers taking the Red Car from Long Beach up to Flower Street in Los Angeles where Uncle Bud and his new wife, Belle, lived. By that time, Bud was working for a machine shop and was a highly skilled machine operator.

Uncle Bud died of coronary heart disease when he was only forty-seven years old. Coach recalls that at dinner his uncle would always have a slice of bread thickly spread with mayonnaise.

He always had that bread with his evening meal—whether it was fried chicken, steak, you name it—he never missed that bread. He wasn't a heavy man—he was not short, not fat, just normal. But we all know that cholesterol doesn't weigh much.

Uncle Bud had three sons with whom Coach spent many of his boyhood years. They were the boys who competed for the attention of Grandma Pearl's thimble.

My cousin Jimmy was the brains of our group; he was a reader. He was a little standoffish—maybe shyer than his brothers. Henry, Jerry, and I were the real hellions. Jimmy was a year older. He ended up as a counselor at a prison—Pelican Bay in Northern California was the last I heard.

I know quite a bit more about my other two cousins, Henry and Jerry. They took after their dad and both became machinists. Henry passed away—he died young, in his late fifties or early sixties. His career had been in machinery, and then he got a credential and was teaching industrial arts at a junior college in the San Diego area—Palomar, I think—for the navy. Henry and I were just a couple of months apart. Jerry was younger—a pregnancy younger—just ten months. He lives in the San Jose area.

Three

Las Vegas

After living in San Bernardino, Peggy, Grandma Pearl, and Uncle Bud moved Tom and his cousins to Las Vegas. They lived in a part of town called Five Points—where five streets intersected. The family moved into and ran the Five Point Motel. Rufus and Uncle Bud bought a garage next door to the motel where they did auto repair. Tom and his brother stayed together in a little motel room with a bed and a bathroom. Most of the other rooms had kitchenettes, as many of the motel patrons were in Las Vegas to establish Nevada's six-week residency so they could get a divorce.

The Five Point was a modest hotel, Craftsman in style, with a gravel parking lot. Each unit had a little porch equipped with two rounded metal chairs, typical of the forties and fifties. The rooms had either one or two beds. Off to one side was a small kitchen with a counter, sink, and icebox. The iceman came at least every other day, especially during the summer.

> We had swamp coolers to help with cooling. But sometimes when it got so hot, you would stand in front of the swamp cooler, and the air it put out didn't feel any cooler than the normal air. No difference; the air was just moving. The fan on the swamp cooler wasn't a propeller but a big roller, a flat blade. They used Excelsior as the cooling product. The water would drip down, and the air from the outside would get pulled through that water. You wouldn't get wet, but it was very humid. They worked—somewhat. They would take the temperature down—probably as effectively as the mist sprayers do now. I remember that it was miserably hot in Las Vegas. We did all our heavy playing either early in the morning or late in the evening, after the sun would go down.

Everyone in the family helped with running the motel. There were no slackers. To this day, Coach says he has no hesitation about doing housework because of his experience there. He says that his wife, Clara, has benefited greatly.

> When my family was in the motel business, everybody pitched in and did everything—from making beds to scrubbing toilets. So, I have never had one problem being a housekeeper. In fact, I have been our primary housekeeper since we've been married. [Laughter and protest from Clara!]

Splish Splash

"Not while you were coaching," she says, and I'd have to agree with that. But when she was teaching and I was coaching, we both worked well together in keeping our house clean.

The Las Vegas of the 1940s was a far different place from the adult amusement park it is now. The family moved to the desert town during World War II. Tom remembers downtown Fremont Boulevard when the Golden Nugget was the big casino and hotel there. Even then, their "Howdy, Partner" neon sign was a Vegas landmark.

> I remember at that time on Fremont Boulevard there were canvas posters with Hitler's picture on one and Tojo's picture on another. The military guys who were in town would throw tomatoes and other things at those posters. When World War II ended, there was a huge celebration in downtown Las Vegas. Perhaps it wasn't as big as I remembered, but as a kid, it seemed almost overwhelming to me.
>
> Another annual celebration in Las Vegas was El Dorado Days with its parade down Fremont Boulevard. Something I really remember was a clown car that popped up on its back tires, and the clown driving could spin the car around. It had a little wheel in the back that the car would balance on. When the driver would goose the car, the front would jump up in the air, the car would spin around, then it would drop back down, and the clown would drive on. Another feature of the parade was a jail that was carried on a big wagon pulled by a truck. They would grab people—mostly adults—right off the street and put them in this jail. They would be in jail for a block or so, and then they would let them out. It's crazy stuff like that that sticks in my mind.

Peggy, Coach's mom, was in poor health for a while in Las Vegas, which caused Tom to miss a great deal of school. As a result, he repeated first grade—a development that made him one of the oldest is his class for the rest of his K–12 school career.

The De Long boys and their cousins continued to enjoy their boyhood in their new hometown. As might be expected, everyone also spent a great deal of time in the water, and Las Vegas was where Coach first came to love diving. But the kids had other adventures as well.

> My brother, sister, and I loved to roller skate. There was an outdoor skating rink real close to the motel; it was open only in the summer. It probably cost ten cents to rent skates and then ten cents to skate. They had piped-in organ music.
>
> We would finish dinner, clean up the kitchen, and then ask my mom if we could go skating. Many times, she would say, "No, we just can't afford that right now." But sometimes she would let us go. And I can remember thinking that was just the greatest treat in the world. We used the old-fashioned key skates that fastened to your hard-soled shoes. There were guys who would skate around on the floor to keep you from going the wrong way or to keep you from speeding, and they always had a skate key around their necks. When your skate came off, they would come and tighten your skate back onto your shoe.
>
> Sure, it was warm, but it would cool off, so it wasn't as hot as it was in the daytime. Everybody loved to go skating in the evening.
>
> There was a swimming pool in Las Vegas where we would swim. That's where I first got interested in diving. Going off the high board there was just the biggest thrill in the world for

me. I would climb way up there and then jump off. To get to even do it, the lifeguard made you swim across the pool—to prove that you could swim, so you were allowed in the deep end. I remember in Las Vegas thinking I was a pretty good swimmer. I just went up to the lifeguard and asked him to let me show him how I could swim, so I could go off the diving board.

The Strip—at the time we first lived in Las Vegas—consisted of the El Rancho Vegas Hotel, which was maybe a quarter mile from where we lived. There were bungalows out in back with the casino up in front. They had a big swimming pool, and we would sneak in. I remember we got into the pool a few times, and then, all of a sudden, the pool attendants recognized who we were. They would just point at us and then point at the gate. They didn't say a word. You'd be out in the middle of the pool and duck under water, and they would just wait. By the time you came up for air, an attendant had come close, and he was glaring at you. So, we would leave. But as I remember, we did get into that pool quite a few times before they started recognizing us.

My stepdad had an old Model A Ford, and we would drive out into the desert to see them building the Flamingo Hotel. What we now know—after all the movies and publicity—is that it was Bugsy Siegel's hotel—and the start of the Mob in Las Vegas. We didn't know that then; it was just an unbelievable hotel that was being built. At Easter, after the hotel was finished, they had an Easter egg hunt and a bubble-blowing contest out at the hotel. I can't exactly remember if I won that contest or not, but I know I got a prize. That had to have been about 1946—it was just after the Flamingo Hotel had opened. So, I was there—taking prizes from the Mob!

Tom's stepdad, Rufus, went to work for the Blue Diamond Gypsum Mine near Las Vegas. Wallboard—drywall—had just been developed. The family left the Five Point Motel and moved closer to Rufus's new place of work. Tom remembers his stepdad coming home and announcing his new job.

He said, "I've bought a ranch; we're going to live on a ranch." Well, I was so excited because I thought we were going to have horses and all sorts of things. We went down there; we lived on New York Avenue, which was near the El Rancho Vegas Hotel. We were the last house on the street—a tiny little house. Out back, there was a little stable where Dad had placed these two ceramic horses, and he said, "These are going to have to be the horses." It was a big disappointment.

Maybe a quarter mile beyond our house into the desert where the railroad tracks were, there were a couple of artesian wells. There was quite a growth of willow and yucca trees there. The bums would be out there—the ones who rode the rails. I can remember that a couple of my friends and I went all over the place collecting materials to help the bums build a fort—a protected place to sleep. I guess that may be my earliest recollection of loving to do things with my hands and to create. We would go out there and help them with the building. Never was I worried in the least—no fear of being molested or taken advantage of. Maybe I was just lucky with the bums I found out there. My folks may have known that I was doing this. Maybe—but I am going to say no.

While living at the New York Avenue house, Coach received his most memorable childhood pet. His maternal aunt May lived in Tampa, Florida. One day, a large, perforated cardboard box arrived in the mail.

Splish Splash

My mother was home, and when she opened the box, an alligator crawled out and just scared the snot out of her! She didn't know how fast it was, and she spent the day—she and the cat—staying a few steps ahead of the alligator. When I got home from school, I named the alligator Slug.

I was so excited about having Slug for a pet. I can remember linking together three or four neighbors' hoses and taking them out what seemed to be a long way but was probably only a couple of hundred feet into the desert. I dug a big hole and filled it full of water for Slug to swim in. When you run water into desert soil, it forms a soapy film. I put Slug in his pond, and right away, he was gone. I searched and searched and couldn't find him. I was worried that he'd crawled off into the desert to die. I had a couple of very sad nights because I could not find Slug. But then the water evaporated and soaked into the ground. I found him buried in the mud.

Oh yeah, Slug lived—and he absolutely loved it. He loved being in that water, and he'd just stay there. After I filled up his little pond a few times, it stopped being so soapy, and I'd watch Slug swimming around out there. Then I'd go out and get him, and he'd come back and stay in my room under the bed.

We fed him a little ball of raw hamburger every two weeks. Alligators have a very, very slow metabolic rate, and they don't eat very much when they are little. When we got Slug, he was fourteen or fifteen inches long. He was a typical little alligator with big, bulgy eyes. Later on, he grew to be almost three feet long.

Four

Arkansas

Tom and his family lived only a year at the little house on New York Avenue. Grandma Pearl had hatched a grand scheme that would take her, Peggy, Bud, and their children far, far away from the hot, dry deserts of the West Coast. Coach's uncle Bud and his wife had separated in Las Vegas, and Bud had custody of the children. It wasn't an amicable separation, and it may have been one of the motivations for Pearl to want to move her family to Arkansas. Also, Pearl had just separated from Mullikin, Rufus's father.

Pearl had grown up in Arkansas. Her dad, Great-Grandpa Lee, still lived there, as did Pearl's sisters Jewel, Ruby, Opal, and Dessie (no one in the family could ever explain where the name Dessie came from). Grandma Pearl decided that her little family could enjoy a better life if they moved home to Arkansas and raised chickens.

> I can remember some magazines that turned up at our house in Las Vegas. They were just newsprint, but they showcased different Arkansas properties, and they had pictures. My grandmother had a whole bunch of them; they must have been sent to her from Arkansas. I can remember looking at the pictures of these farms, thinking they were just the coolest places ever.

Slug the alligator moved with the family to Arkansas, where his saga continued.

> We lost Slug on our trip from Las Vegas to Arkansas. We were sure that Slug had crawled out when we had stopped someplace along the way. We were all resigned that he was lost forever, but then when we had been in Arkansas several days, my dad was driving someplace, and he heard Slug croak. He'd crawled under the front seat of our 1941 Chevy. Dad looked under the seat of the car, and there was Slug. He had a wound in his hind leg from being caught in the springs. But otherwise, he was just fine.

Coach and his family found life very different in Arkansas from San Bernardino and Las Vegas. The climate and scenery of the Ozarks were not only different but also very rural.

Splish Splash

Up until that point, we'd always lived in town. San Bernardino was in town. Las Vegas—as rural as it was at that time—seemed to me to be a big place. When we moved to Arkansas, we were out in the middle of nowhere. Man, it was the Stone Age!

My grandmother had purchased a farm and acreage—she footed the whole venture. The farm wasn't a chicken ranch at the time she bought it. It did have a big, traditional barn. But then my uncle and my dad and other relatives from back there built three big, long chicken houses. When we first moved to Arkansas, we had no electricity at all. The first electricity that came went into the chicken houses. If you turn on the lights and get the chickens up, then they will get up at four in the morning. With long days, you could get them to lay twice a day.

So began Coach's time as a chicken rancher. It proved a good life for the little family, and had tragedy not occurred, there might well have never been a De Long aquatic dynasty at Foothill High School. Coach became very involved and interested in chickens.

I went to school for two years in Arkansas—third and fourth grades. My memories of those years are pretty good. I didn't realize it at the time, but the whole family was putting in a good work effort there. It wasn't considered chores. It was just an expectation that everyone pitched in and did what had to be done. We got up in the morning, and there were always things to do. I still had playtime, but there was also work time.

You bet I collected eggs. Of course, these were fertilized eggs, and the hens were very protective. Oh, it was war. And the roosters were mean. They'd come after you.

I remember getting a broom [the bristles were made out of wheat then]—I cut all the bristles off to where they were sewn up at the top. Then I cut the broom handle so it was about club size. That was my protection when I went in the chicken yards. One time, I accidentally killed a rooster. I must have broken the bird's neck. Then I attempted to hide the carcass behind the barn—the one that served as our main chicken house. My dad found the body, and I had to pay for the rooster! It seemed like it took weeks of my allowance. That was a lesson I learned the hard way.

We had chicken hawks. You tried to keep the hens quiet because if they ran, then their eggs would get blood spots in them. So, when the hens all took off for the chicken house, you knew there was a chicken hawk. You'd look, and it would be way up there. The roosters would drop their wings down, and they'd turn their heads to the side, looking up with one eye at the hawk. They would fluff themselves up to look like turkeys and walk with their wings dragging behind them. They would stay out in the middle of the yard while the hens went into the chicken houses. These roosters were huge—they weighed probably fifteen pounds—and the chicken hawks couldn't pick them up.

Life on the chicken farm had its own beauty and lessons from nature.

We had two thousand white Wyandotte roosters and eight thousand Rhode Island Red hens. It was absolutely a beautiful sight. I can remember the sun being on those birds, and the light would reflect off their feathers. The roosters' skin was completely red. The roosters at the bottom of the pecking order were easy to tell because their red skin would be showing through. We had to separate them out, and we'd try them in a different yard. There were about three of four different yards; all ten thousand birds weren't together. So, the roosters at the bottom of the pecking order would start to lose their feathers. That's where the idea from psychology of a pecking order comes from—it comes from chickens.

My mom would keep the roosters at the bottom of the pecking order in our backyard. No, they weren't pets—they were Sunday dinner! We ate a lot of chicken dinners in Arkansas. Fried chicken and mashed potatoes and all that good stuff. I never got tired of it. It probably wasn't very healthy, but oh, it was very good.

Chicken farming is hard work, and great skill and care is needed to be successful. Grandma Pearl recognized that her family had "the right stuff" to make a go of it. She split up the family into two camps. Peggy and her family ran the egg business; Bud and his crew were in Fayetteville raising poulets.

We were taking between one hundred fifty and one hundred seventy-five dozen eggs a week to the hatchery. The concept was to take the eggs and sell them to the hatchery. My grandmother and uncle in Fayetteville started raising poulets. They would buy the baby chicks from the hatchery and raise them for twelve weeks; then they were sold for chicken dinner. What was going to happen—what the plan was—is we were going to build our own hatchery, and we were going to do the whole chicken cycle—have the whole thing.

As Coach describes what it took to raise chickens and sell their eggs, one can see the beginnings of the observational skills that marked his success as an athletic coach.

To transport the eggs, we had a 1946 Chevy with a trailer. I can remember my dad bought some special springs and that trailer just floated! This was before foam rubber, and he had some special padding he would put down to reduce road shock. In wintertime, we had to cover the trailer with a big tarp so the eggs wouldn't freeze. The eggs themselves were in egg boxes. We used and reused these boxes that go two dozen in a layer. You put a cardboard separator between each layer. I think we'd put six or seven dozen eggs in a box. Then that box went into the trailer.

Eggs that go to a hatchery have to be within a tolerance of a certain weight. If the eggs are too small or too large, then they won't hatch. There are mutations and all sorts of problems. When we'd arrive at the hatchery, there would be two or three guys pulling the eggs out of our cartons so fast it would make your head swim. They'd tap the eggs—they'd take two eggs and tap them together. Unless the eggs made a particular sound, they were no good.

The rejected eggs were called cull eggs. Typically, out of one hundred twenty dozen eggs, we would have ten or twelve dozen that would be culls. After they culled them, they would set the eggs on this machine that had rotating lifters to lift each egg. If the eggs were a certain weight, then the machine would tip them, and they would roll down this slight incline—so slow that they wouldn't break if they bumped into one another. Then there were people down at the other end putting the eggs on a conveyer belt. They would disappear down the conveyer belt and then go into incubators. The eggs would go into trays—maybe eighteen or twenty-four, I can't remember—then they would slide the trays under lights that create the perfect temperature for those eggs to incubate. Then they hatch. And that's what happened at the hatchery.

But the eggs in the lifters that were too light or too heavy would get dumped on the cull side. My job was to take the cull eggs and sort them by size. That's how you get small, medium, and large eggs. In those days, we had only two sizes of eggs on the market: small and large. All the mediums went to the hatchery. On the way home from the hatchery in Fayetteville, we would stop at three or four different stores that bought eggs from us. Today, the eggs we buy at the store are raised for consumption, and they are not fertilized. In those days, all the eggs were fertilized, and the ones for consumption were the culls from the hatchery.

While the little family was investing their time and money into the chicken business, Coach's mother, Peggy, continued to sew everyone's clothes. The family's new business enterprise allowed her to acquire some fabric for free.

When we had the chicken ranch, the chicken feed came in bags. I think they were forty-five pound bags. They were big enough that if you got two bags with the same print, then you had enough cloth to make dresses. Many of my mom's and sister's dresses were made from feed bags. The sacks came in different prints and were made of a cotton-type material. So, when the feed truck would come, we would race down and put dibs on the prints we wanted! We had ten thousand hens, and we had feed deliveries every ten days to two weeks. But you know, making clothes from feed sacks happened all over America; my wife has some of her baby clothes that were made for her from feed sacks when she was growing up in Colorado.

Of course, it wasn't all work and no play for Coach, Paul, Marjorie, and the cousins in Fayetteville. Everyone looked forward to the times when the families could get together.

My grandmother had her place just outside of Fayetteville, and my uncle Bud and my three cousins lived with her. Visiting my grandmother was always a fun time. My cousins would also come down to our place, which was about twenty miles away. We would spend weekends in Fayetteville, and they then would come have sleepovers with us.

One of the big activities, if it was too cold to be outside, was Monopoly. We played like crazy. We kept our game board on a big piece of plywood, and we would slide it under the bed when we had to stop playing. Then we'd pull it out in the morning. We had marathon games that would last two or three days. That was a lot of fun. It never seemed like we wanted for much in those days.

While we were in Arkansas, we kept our canned goods in a little shed. My grandmother canned for as long as I can remember—as far back as Las Vegas. She always had a place where she kept the jars. My brother's favorite was the pears, and I loved peaches. Every once in a while, my brother would sneak out of our room, and he would get a jar of pears and one of peaches. Then he and I would eat them at night. The next day, we would have to get rid of the evidence.

Our Christmas tree was always a very big deal in our family. We made many of our own decorations. We did have a lot of old decorations, too. The first electric lights I remember on our

Christmas tree were in Las Vegas. We had bubble lights—this was way back when they first came out. I think my grandmother bought them. We would string popcorn for the tree and make chains of construction paper rings. The big thing back then was icicles. They were made out of tinfoil and came in packages in which the icicles were draped over a cardboard sleeve. You would take them out of the package and hang them over all the branches. Well, it just took forever. Finally, you would start taking two or three icicles at a time and start tossing them on the tree. My mom used to get so mad. And then there was a product called Angel Hair. It was spun glass, and you would drape the Angel Hair over the tree after everything was decorated. Then the lights on the tree would starburst through the Angel Hair. It created a really neat effect.

When we were in Arkansas, we would go out and find a perfect Christmas tree. We would start looking early—and of course, we had only a couple of Christmases there. But I can remember finding trees and marking them—saying this is the tree we're going to get. We'd always go cut it down right after Thanksgiving.

We celebrated Christmas on Christmas Eve for some reason. I don't think I started celebrating Christmas on Christmas morning until I got married and Clara and I had our own family. Thanksgiving dinner was always a big dinner at our house. We always had my sister, brother, mom and dad, grandmother, uncle, and cousins—it was a big family occasion.

And then there was Slug the alligator. For a time, he adapted to life in the Ozarks.

We had a big footstool with a top that opened. I would put Slug in there at night with a bunch of newspapers. We had no heat in the house. In the morning, I would take him out, and he would literally be stiff; he was curled up in the footstool. I would put him under our kitchen stove, which was a wood-burning stove. He'd get warm under there, and pretty soon, he'd come crawling out.

One day, I put Slug in the cows' watering trough, but he terrified the cows, and I was told not to do that.

Slug made it through our first winter in Arkansas. But one day, I found him in the trough, and he was dead. We never knew what happened. I think there was some kind of contamination in the water—something that was toxic to his system but not to anything else. I should have listened to my dad and not let him go swimming again.

So, that was the end of Slug. We buried him, and his final resting place is Arkansas. He is an Arkie.

Newcastle disease is a serious bird virus. Although it has now been controlled in this country, there remains no cure. It is highly contagious and spreads through the birds' droppings and nasal discharge. The virus can also penetrate eggshells and infect the embryo. It can survive for several weeks in warm and humid environments, and indefinitely in frozen material.

Newcastle remains a dangerous disease for birds. The US government still closely scrutinizes exotic birds—like parrots and parakeets—when they are shipped into the country. They don't want those birds coming in and infecting the fowl population, which includes chickens and turkeys.

We had probably been in Arkansas a year and a half when our birds got Newcastle disease. I remember that these men came to our place, and they had a bunch of small chicken coops—the kind used to transport chickens in trucks. We put our chickens in the little coops, and the men would pull each chicken out, lift up a wing, and collect a blood sample.

They used a tool that looked like a wand you'd use to blow bubbles, only these were made out of stainless steel. One end had a point they would use to stick the chicken in a vein. Then they would use the little wand to get a little film of blood. They would take that film and put it on a big glass sheet that was gridded into squares. When they touched the wand to the glass, the blood sample would create a circle on the glass. Then they would band the chicken on its leg and send it into another pen. After they had tested one cage full of chickens—maybe twelve or so—they would immerse the glass into a solution. When they lifted it up, if a chicken had the disease, then its sample would turn a particular color—I remember it being purple.

When they tested our chickens, they would hold up the glass, and if there were twelve squares, then I remember nine or so would be purple. What they were trying to do was cull out the diseased chickens. They would put the disease-free chickens in one area and the ones who had Newcastle in another area. I can remember my mom crying because some of the grids when they were pulled up had every square showing purple. As the testing went on, it became more and more apparent that our entire flock was heavily, heavily infected.

The symptoms, as I understand them, are similar to polio. The disease affects the central nervous system. I can remember that some of our chickens would get weird; they couldn't walk and would stumble, their heads would be turned to one side or the other. Their wings would droop—and I can't remember exactly how it happened—but eventually, they would just die. I remember we sold the birds that weren't infected to Swanson's in Fayetteville, Arkansas.

The decision to move to Phoenix happened rapidly.

Everything happened in a period of maybe a couple of months. We sold the chicken farm, and as the matriarch, my grandmother was the person who headed up the process. I think we left for Phoenix after school let out in the spring of 1949.

Before we moved to Phoenix from Arkansas, I remember we killed and butchered a pig that I had raised. I wasn't in 4-H, but I know I was going to enter this pig in some kind of contest. I had won the pig at a greased pole climbing in the little town of Westfork. He was just a little guy when I got him. In the end, my dad shot him in the head and then butchered him before we moved to Phoenix. That was really sad for me. Clara has similar stories about some of her animals that she'd raised for 4-H.

Another thing I remember about moving from Arkansas to Phoenix had to do with canned goods. My mother and grandmother did a lot of canning; they canned everything. When we were going into one of the states on our trip west—it may have been New Mexico—the border people refused to let us take our canned goods into the state. To this day, I do not understand why. But my family felt that the state inspection station men wanted the fruits for themselves. I can remember my dad going over to a trash can and breaking all of the glass jars into it. If they weren't going to let us take the fruit into the state, then there was no way he was going to let them have it, either. I remember there were several cases—many, many bottles of preserves.

Five

Phoenix

When the family moved to Phoenix, Grandma Pearl purchased a motel in a residential area. It was group of small cottage-like houses facing a courtyard. Later, Pearl would buy a motel on Van Buren Avenue about a block and a half from the capitol building in downtown Phoenix. It was called Green's Motel. In Phoenix, Peggy and Bud's families again lived together at the motels. Rufus was pursuing a career as an upholsterer. Peggy and Bud also worked, and Grandma Pearl was caretaker for all the children.

> I remember that while we were living there, we had spaghetti a lot. My cousins and I were allowed to eat in a separate room in the kitchen. The four of us would slurp our spaghetti and see who could get the most stripes across their faces! We were almost all the same age. We would sit there and laugh and slurp spaghetti and get stripes all over our faces.
>
> My brother and I used to ride the bus in Phoenix. We didn't have a television set in our home yet. So, we would ride once a week to a furniture store that had a television set in the front window. They had a speaker outside, and my brother and I would go there to watch *The Lone Ranger* every week. It wasn't an easy bus ride, either. We rode the bus, got a transfer, and took another bus to get to this furniture store to watch *The Lone Ranger*. It was a two- or three-hour trip to watch a thirty-minute show.

Coach was now out of the primary grades, and school became a more important focus. He discovered a lifelong interest in art and also that he did not particularly enjoy English or writing. He had a memorable teacher at Capitol Elementary School, Mr. Painter, who coached him in baseball and also supervised the student crossing guards. Coach learned important lessons about preparation, responsibility, and compassion from Mr. Painter.

> Mr. Painter was awesome. But sixth grade might be why I never wanted to pursue baseball. I remember getting hit in the head with a baseball bat; I was playing catcher. I think I was knocked out—I remember I had a bump on my head about the size of a person's hand. Mr. Painter took me home after the accident. We lived only a block from the school at Green's Motel on Van Buren Avenue.

Splish Splash

In sixth grade, I became a student crossing guard. On Van Buren—I thought this was the biggest deal in the whole world—there was an apparatus with a wooden arm that came out and extended into the street. The crossing guards got to unlock the arm and operate it. When the arm was extended, it went out into the first lane of traffic, maybe ten feet into the street. There was a big stop sign at the end of it. It was like a railroad crossing, only smaller. The arm was counterbalanced. There was a handle, and when you pulled up on it, the counterbalance allowed the arm to drop down. Before we were allowed to even operate this device, we had to practice. There wasn't a traffic light at that intersection, and Van Buren was one of the main, busy streets in Phoenix. You had to be really careful that you didn't hit a car. So, you'd have to wait for a break in traffic before you could lower the arm to allow kids to cross the street.

All the crossing guards had envelope-style army hats that always had to be pointed slightly to the left. Then we had a red jacket with a little patch that read "Crossing Guard." We couldn't give out tickets, but if anybody violated a traffic rule when the crossing guards had the arm down, then it was possible for the drivers to be issued a ticket. We really thought that we were important. And Mr. Painter told us that what we were doing was really, really important.

Coach had his first paying jobs in Phoenix. Not surprisingly, he quickly became an entrepreneur.

I got my first job in Phoenix at a delicatessen, where I was to watch the roast beef that was cooking in the back kitchen. I also got to work behind the counter a little bit. This all happened when I was twelve years old. I had earned money other ways before, but working in the deli was the first time I felt I'd held a responsible position.

The way I first earned real money in Phoenix was by shining shoes. I got a shoeshine box, and my grandmother helped me pay for the materials to fill it up—a brush, polish, and polish rags that would snap. I had a little strap on my shoulder to help me carry my shoeshine box.

I would go down Van Buren toward downtown where there were all these used car lots. I would shine shoes for ten cents, and the salesmen were good customers. So, I would make my way down Van Buren shining shoes. By the time I got downtown, I had enough money to go to the movie and to buy a drink and popcorn. On the way back from the movie, I would buy myself a meal at the little coffee shop beside our motel. I would go in there and have a hamburger, French fries, and a milk shake. Shoe shinning was a good little business.

Coach's stepdad, Rufus, attended trade school in Phoenix to become an upholsterer. That career did not work out as he had intended, so he then decided to reenlist in the navy, which precipitated the family's return to California. Grandma Pearl stayed on in Phoenix. Uncle Bud and his family moved back to California at a different time. Coach and his family moved to Long Beach in 1952. He was fourteen years old and in seventh grade.

Coach's Mom, Peggy

Splish Splash

Peggy and Uncle Bud

Tom De Long with Sharon Hastings

Grandma Pearl

Coach during family motel days

Splish Splash

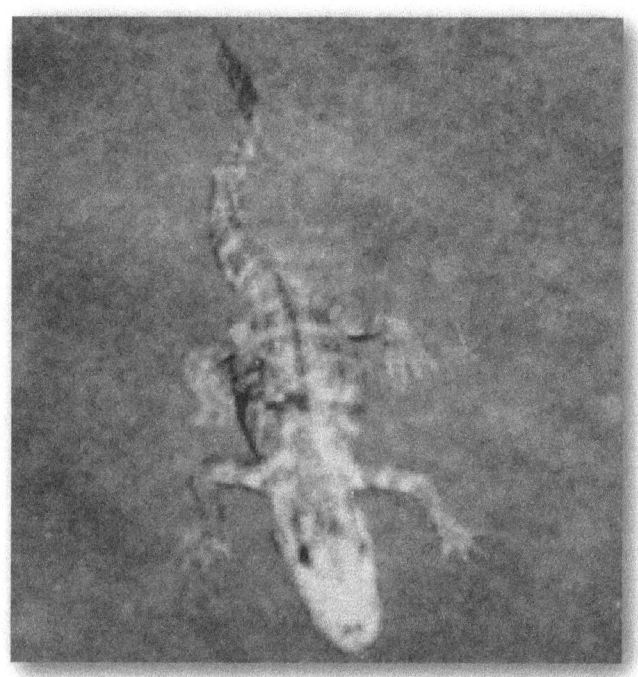

Slug, the alligator

Mr. Painter's Crossing Guards
(Coach is top row, fifth from the left)

Paul, Marjorie and Coach

Paul Delong

Coach with trophy from Long Beach Soap Box Derby

Six

Long Beach

Rufus was stationed in San Diego, and Peggy got a job at the Foremost Clothing Factory in Long Beach, where she sewed blue jeans. The family lived behind a used car lot in a row of cottages, almost like a little row motel. There were six or seven of these small houses, all built sometime in the 1920s. The car lot that fronted their new home opened up to Long Beach Boulevard, which was then called American Avenue.

Long Beach was a teenager's paradise in the early fifties: great weather, the beach, proximity to Los Angeles, and lots of kids for friends. Coach continued his entrepreneurial practices to finance his movie and popcorn habit. He also developed innovative ways to score a meal after a long day at the beach.

> When we lived in Long Beach, we would go down to the beach and collect pop bottles. If they had any sand in them at all, then the liquor store would only give you a penny. So, we would go to the showers at the back of the beach and rinse them out. Then you could get two cents a bottle. With the money we got, we would have enough to go to the movies and have popcorn and a drink. This would take maybe an hour of collecting bottles down at the beach.
>
> One of the things we used to do—my friend Glenn Humphrey and I—was to make a list of ten items, five of which you could eat. When we were coming home from the beach and were ravishingly hungry, we would go on either side of the street, and we would tell people we were on a scavenger hunt. We would knock on doors and say, "We need a button, an empty aspirin bottle, half a peanut butter sandwich, and a piece of red thread." Some people would hesitate—"Well, I don't know. Oh, wait a minute; I'll make you a peanut butter sandwich"—or we'd ask for an apple or any kind of hard candy, but we would always slip in two or three items that you could eat. We really thought we were getting away with something. I am sure we didn't fool anyone. Here we are in bathing suits with sand all over our feet and T-shirts on—and we're in a scavenger hunt party? Yeah, right!

Early on in Long Beach, Coach developed an avid interest in Soap Box Derby racing. A Chevy dealer, Cormier Chevrolet, on American Avenue, was participating in a national dealership program that paid for the ball bearing wheels for kids who were building Soap Box Derby cars. The wheels were red and beautiful. Soap Box Derby cars using them would be displayed in the dealership window. Coach was hooked. A neighbor lady lent him her unused, detached single-car garage as a workshop. It was blazing hot in the summertime, and the fourteen-year-old had few tools. Still, he managed to build cars.

> No one helped me build the car. Even at that time, some of the cars—especially those that made it to Akron, Ohio, for the national championships—kids had their dads help. We raced at Griffith Park in Los Angeles. At that race were three or four cars sponsored by Cormier Chevrolet. They took our cars on a flatbed truck to the event at the park. I thought it didn't get any better than that.
>
> There was a hill at the park marked off with three lanes. They had a little ramp, and an apparatus came up and held the nose of the three cars racing. It was kind of like the start of a motocross race. Once those nose holders dropped, the cars took off. Of course, there were no motors; the cars were just coasting. But the ramp gets you going, and then you go on to asphalt—then it's down a hill. They didn't make the hill really, really fast, but the cars did get going.
>
> I got a trophy with the second car I built, but I didn't win overall. If you won your division, then you went someplace else for a bigger race. Then those cars got to go to Akron.

There were some tougher neighborhoods in Long Beach, and some of the kids from the west side of the city went to Washington Junior High. A year older than most of the kids in his class, Coach was pretty physically mature by the time he got to Washington. Some of the mean kids thought to take him on. They clocked him against a locker one day. That's when Coach decided he needed to be strong enough to defend himself.

> On Long Beach Boulevard, at Sixth Street, there was a Sears department store. In the exercise section, they had dumbbells. My friend and I would go in there, and we would do arm curls—like we were trying out the weights. The sales guy in that department knew what we were doing, but he never kicked us out. So, we would go in there and do almost a full workout—lifting weights—acting like we were just shopping.

But the free workouts weren't enough, so Coach joined the YMCA near his house.

> When I went in to join the Y, there were some expenses. There was an initiation fee and monthly dues—maybe six dollars. I didn't have the money to do that. So, I went in and talked to one of the guys I'd befriended, and I got a job as a towel boy. I would issue towels for a period of time—kind of like a job, but I didn't get paid for it. I got my membership in exchange for the work.

At the Y, Coach got interested in Greco Roman wrestling. It's an Olympic sport and differs from freestyle wrestling because wrestling the shoulders of the opponent past vertical to the mat scores a "win." This type of wrestling emphasizes balance, and there is a lot of Judo to it.

I remember I got on the wrestling team, and I got wrestling tights, which I thought were just the greatest. They came down to the middle of the thigh. It was one piece with no sleeves. Gosh, I thought that was the best.

Coach's first wrestling tournament—his first athletic competition in any sport—was in Pasadena in 1952. He'd done well at the Y in Long Beach, and in his words, he thought he was "pretty hot stuff."

Guess what? My first opponent was blind. I'm thinking, "Oh, this poor guy. He doesn't have a chance." When you're wrestling someone who is blind, the only difference from a regular match is that he's allowed to put his hand on your shoulder. This guy put his hand on my shoulder, and the official said, "Ready. Wrestle." It seemed to me that in like one point two seconds I was flat on my back, and it was over! So, that was my first experience in organized sports.

Oh man, it was humbling. But I watched the rest of the tournament, and each time the blind guy wrestled, the person he was wrestling lasted—well, some lasted a little bit longer than I did—but he won the whole event handily. I found out later that this guy was known as a very skilled wrestler. He knew just by touching you what you were doing, where you were going, and what your move might be. He was truly amazing.

It was at the YMCA that Coach first began gymnastics. Although the Y didn't have a team, his junior high did, and he competed for his school. Gymnastics at the Y, however, provided an easy transition to diving—and the YMCA had a swimming pool.

There was coed swimming once a week at the Y. Being on the diving board is a good opportunity to show off. The Y had only a one-meter diving board. It was an old aluminum buckboard—which is what they were called—and they were noisy. The Y pool was in the basement with windows that were foggy glass block. Everything in the room—I think, including the ceiling—was tile. It was so noisy when you would bounce that diving board. It would echo in there like being inside a bell that was being rung. When you walked out and bounced the diving board, everybody knew it. There was a dive happening! So, I started diving at coed rec swimming night at the Y. I'd gotten pretty interested in girls by then.

Beyond gymnastics, Coach also competed in track in junior high as a high jumper. But gymnastics was his first love. In ninth grade, the family moved to a new home in Long Beach, and Coach had to transfer from Washington to Franklin Junior High. The coach and parents at Lindbergh were excited to have him join their team.

Team loyalty has always been really important to me, and I think it stems from that transfer I made in junior high. One thing that irritates the heck out of me is when I watch a professional football game, and they'll talk about a player and say, for example, that he's a former Seattle Seahawk who now plays for the Denver Broncos. I hate that. I believe there needs to be an allegiance to the team. In those days, I don't think I had any choice about transferring. When you moved, you had to attend the school whose attendance area you were in. But suddenly, I was competing against my former teammates at Washington—and that didn't feel right.

Seven

Diving

There was no diving program at either junior high school or at the YMCA. Coach taught himself as he tried to impress the girls at coed swim night. He began diving in earnest at Long Beach Poly High School and had two fine coaches. But then he had a star-crossed encounter: he had the opportunity to meet Pat McCormick.

> I met Pat in 1955 at a diving meet. She was preparing for the 1956 Olympics in Melbourne. Glenn, her husband, was the Olympic coach. She was diving at the meet, and I started talking with her. I clicked immediately with Glenn, who was coaching her there. They lived around the corner from my sister. When we discovered this, they said, "Oh good. Now, we've got a built-in babysitter." I began babysitting for them, and they took an interest in my diving career.

The McCormicks trained at the LA Athletic Club. It was an interesting venue, and Coach has a crystal-clear memory of the first time he dove there.

> The swimming pool at the LA Athletic Club is on the sixth floor. I really remember my first time on the high board. As I was standing there getting ready to do a practice approach, I looked over through the window down to the street. Here I am ten feet above the pool and six floors above the street! What a freaky experience!

Four coaches influenced Coach in high school: Glenn McCormick, Wally Rogers, Dick Peck, and famed Olympian Dr. Sammy Lee. They had different coaching styles, and each was a different influence.

> Glenn was a taskmaster coach, expecting you to sacrifice your body to try and learn what you had to learn. And it hurt. But I was pretty fearless in those days and didn't really have a lot of trouble handling the pain in missing dives.
>
> I had two diving coaches in high school. One was Wally Rogers. The other one, who had been a diver and was a volunteer coach, was Dick Peck.
>
> They were two different sorts of coaches. Wally Rogers was more of a technician; Dick Peck coached by a trial-and-error method! Spin until you hit the water. Or he would call us out of

dives—which I learned to do—and I used this technique a lot when I was coaching. This method taught you timing and how to spot the water. Rogers had a more technical approach that focused on diving mechanics. He would have us rehearse the dive in our minds before we tried it—create a mental picture. Then he would have us practice by repetition; we would do twenty front dives and then twenty back dives. By the end of the workout, you were completely shot because there were so many times up the ladder—let alone what it took to do all those dives.

As a coach, Sammy Lee was a real master of technique—and teaching technique. He was just a marvelous person, a wonderful personality. I always wondered how it would be for an Olympic champion to coach someone who had considerably less talent. And Sammy Lee did a great job with whomever he was coaching.

Sammy Lee invited Coach out to dive at his first swim school on Lincoln Avenue in Anaheim. There were several really good divers diving there, including Bob Webster and Jack Fury. This happened Coach's sophomore year at Poly, after he had placed fifth in CIF. Sammy Lee was at the meet, and he encouraged the young diver to come out and practice with him. Coach went whenever he could.

He was working with Jack Fury and Bobby Webster. Bobby Webster was the 1960 Olympic champion in Rome on the ten meter. Sammy had us do training on the trampoline. He had a belt that was a ring—the size of a small Hula-Hoop—with a belt connected inside of it. Once you put it on, you could twist inside of it. The outside of the ring had two clips that were attached to a line connected to two poles on either side of the trampoline. A spotter would hold the two lines as you would jump. You learned how to do forward twisting dives, backward twisting dives, and reverse twisting dives. It was a good way to learn timing.

It's like the Olympic skiing event—freestyle—where they go up the ramp and then do phenomenal moves once they're up in the air—just mind-boggling. Those skiers learn those moves over a swimming pool or at a lake and use techniques similar to those we used on the trampoline with Sammy Lee.

Coach had a rich diving career, first at Long Beach Poly and then at Long Beach City College. The technology then was more primitive than it is for divers today.

The list—as it's called—of dives that you do was somewhat limited in those days by the diving boards you used. My earliest recollection of boards was a wooden one made out of something almost like a dock. They were covered with cocoa mat—so the board wouldn't just be slick wood.

The first aluminum diving board that I ever dove on was called a buckboard. Those boards had nuts and bolts in them to hold them together, and they were loud. They would rattle, and if you were in an indoor pool, then the noise was just horrible. If you ever got to the point where you had a nice smooth approach and you could spring the board without it making a lot of noise, then it seemed like you would always score higher. The less noise, the higher the score. Then they started putting pool towels under the fulcrum roller to dampen the sound. The fulcrums, I believe, were made of hard rubber. That helped muffle the sound, especially in the indoor pools.

Splish Splash

In those days, the dives themselves went by different names.

> My least favorite dives were spinning reverse dives. I liked them least because of the diving boards of the time. You really couldn't get the height off the board then that you can get now.
>
> My favorite dives were anything frontward—forward dives: swan dives, jackknife, one and a half pike, two and a half pike—all the forward spinning dives. The inward dive back in those days was called a cutaway. The reverse dives were called gainers. That changed in the late sixties to early seventies. They formally changed the cutaway to an inward dive; the gainers were changed to reverse dives.

A particular thrill for any serious diver is to step up from the one- and three-meter diving boards and to start diving off the ten-meter tower.

> When you start tower diving, I think everyone had some apprehensions. But once you do a few dives, you learn that the impact into the water is not dramatically different from what you've experienced on the three-meter board. The difference is that there is no spring on the tower; you have to do more of a tumbling takeoff. I enjoyed tower diving; I absolutely loved it while I was doing it. I dove platform for probably four years; I even did a little bit of it at the Air Force Academy when I was at the University of Denver.

Diving is a beautiful sport, and when done well, it looks almost effortless. All divers, however, have war stories.

> I do remember a bad splat. I had just started diving ten meter. I was at the Los Angeles Coliseum pool and was learning a handstand/cut through. What you learn first is to just do a handstand, and then as you fall off, you do a reverse dive. You don't want to fall much before you start the reverse; if you fall too far now, then your body wants to keep going in the direction it's going, which would take you into a forward spin. So, obviously, you have to leave the tower—you can't just stand there—but then you have to immediately go into the reverse dive.
>
> When you first learn the dive, it's pretty frightening. You're looking down at the water from your handstand, and if the pool isn't agitated, then you're not only looking down the thirty-three feet to the surface of the water but also an additional eighteen feet to the bottom of the pool. So, at the beginning, it's a frightening experience. You have a spotter up on the tower with you to help you so you can get a feel for doing a handstand up there. You can't throw a handstand up there; you have to be able to do the handstand in a controlled fashion so that you can place yourself right at the edge of the platform. And then you have to maintain three seconds of balance before you start the actual dive. If you just go up and off, then the judges will knock you for a deduction.
>
> Well, this day, I got knocked out. The first or second time, I was trying the dive going in headfirst rather than feetfirst. I missed the dive, stretched, and landed flat on my back. All I remember is that I woke up on the deck. They had to rescue me from the water. That was typical in a wipeout like that.

Tom De Long with Sharon Hastings

> You can do some very serious damage off a ten-meter tower. You can rupture a spleen if you are completely lost and miss a dive. In some ways, I was lucky with the splat I took, but I can tell you that you don't want to do it twice. I was bruised all over my body. But everybody goes through something like that.

Coach explains that new technology helps current divers have a better sense of the water when they do platform diving—and better protection if they make a mistake.

> Nowadays, they have what they call a bubbler. They were developed in Canada. There is a ring on the bottom of the pool linked to a foot pedal on the pool deck. Just as a diver leaves the tower, the coach steps on the pedal—they work the timing just right—and the diver lands in a sea of bubbles. So, now it's literally possible for a diver to land completely flat and not get hurt. The bubbles break the surface tension, which is what hurts the diver in a bad dive.
>
> You don't even need to hit as hard as I did to have a problem with surface tension when you're diving. If you enter the water with your hands apart—and your head is the first thing to hit—then you will feel it. One of the first things you learn as a diver is that the tips of your fingers don't hurt, no matter how fast you're traveling. In fact, some divers will hold their fingers together but flatten their hands as they hit the water—they hit the water first with the palms of their hands, which explodes the surface tension and makes room for the body to follow. That's how divers do it when they enter the water with absolutely zero splash. Of course, now those doggone divers are all so tiny—there's no need for them to make a very big hole in the water at all. When you do see a big splash now, it's because the diver has really missed his or her entry on the dive.

The mishap at the LA Coliseum was not the only one Coach would sustain. Other diving injuries involved hitting the board or the bottom of the pool.

> I'd hit the board with my hands doing a reverse spin dive coming out and then slapping the end of it with my hands. Then I had a lot of dislocated fingers diving into shallow pools. The reason divers hit the board—and some of the hits are pretty scary—is because of improper takeoff.

Coach enjoyed a lot of success as a high school diver. He was league champion two of the three years in high school. He made the CIF finals all three years.

> My favorite board was always the three meter. I had the greatest success on it. My most difficult dive was probably a forward double twisting one and a half. It was a dive I liked, and I scored well with it. I liked diving all through high school, but I probably had my most significant success when I got to Long Beach City College. Diving steps up quite a bit at the junior college level.

Eight

Football

Diving was not Coach's only sport in high school and college. Arguably, it was his "second" sport. That's because Coach played football—and he was good. He started when he was in eighth grade when he turned out for the Signal Hill Bulldogs, a junior high flag football team. But this was Long Beach—a Southern California legacy football town. So even at the junior high level, there were many very good athletes, and the competition was fierce.

Throughout his football career, Coach played offensive guard and defensive noseguard, or middle linebacker.

> In those days—all the way through college—football players played both ways—offense and defense. Through my whole high school career, I rarely left the playing field. When the ball turned over, I became a linebacker on defense. Then when we got the ball back, I played guard on offense.
>
> You had to be in shape. Everybody hated wind sprints, but we did wind sprints like crazy. It was all part of our expectations and certainly the expectations of our coaches. Most everybody played two positions.

As a sophomore—his first year at Long Beach Poly—Coach played junior varsity. He played varsity his junior and senior years. Balancing his body weight to both dive and play football was challenging.

> My sophomore year, I think I weighed one hundred seventy-five pounds. I would always gain weight for football and lose weight for diving. Having spent some time wrestling—wrestlers are famous for being able to quickly lose weight—I already knew how to do this. I always dove at about one hundred seventy-five or one hundred eighty pounds. Then I would play football at as much as two hundred five pounds. I did it through a very strict diet; I cut out certain foods. I used water pills, too. We did some things then that would now not be considered the healthiest regimens.

Coach remembers his high school coaches and his teammates. The quality of his coaching was high, and his fellow players were gifted.

Tom De Long with Sharon Hastings

Doc Cure was one of the coaches I really remember. He was head coach my junior and senior years. Ray Morey was my junior varsity coach. Another coach, Dave Levy—with whom I'm still in contact—ended up coaching at USC and then was their offensive coordinator/defensive coordinator. He went on to be assistant coach for several professional teams.

We did have a good football team. Jim Smith was a fantastic player. Henry Andrews, Dee Andrews, Matthew Shipp—they all ended up playing beyond high school.

The list of Long Beach Poly players going on to play in the National Football League is very long—they have had more NFL players than any other high school in the country. Many of the strong players at the University of Southern California have come from Poly. There is a very tight connection between the two schools. Everybody who's played at Poly feels a part of the tradition.

Coach loved football—the practices, his team, his coaches. Some of what he learned in the team sport of football he later utilized coaching swimming, diving, and water polo.

As I look back, I remember thinking, "Hurry up, sixth period, so I can get out to practice." I also loved game day. Before the game, we would sometimes have team dinners. We'd eat at four p.m., and when we returned to the locker room, Coach would darken it and make us all contemplate the upcoming game. He wanted us to put ourselves in a good place, and that quiet time helped us do that.

Some of the guys on the team were so funny. During quiet time, somebody would make some remark, and we'd all start laughing. The coach would come in and just rip on everybody. It would remind me of the times my cousins would visit for overnighters, and we'd start giggling, and then my mother or my grandmother would come in—it was a very similar situation.

I think my time playing football did help later as I was coaching—from a team standpoint. I always really loved to make my swimming team feel like a team and not just a group of individuals. Esprit de corps is important whenever you put a group together.

When I first started coaching water polo, I darkened the room and gave my players quiet time. We used to go on the stage in the gym. I would put the kids in there and turn the lights out. This was in the early 1970s. It was a serious time, and the guys just ate it up. When we had night events, we had team dinners, too.

When I started coaching the Foothill girls' teams, we also had some fun things that we did. We often had team breakfasts before big events. Somebody would host a breakfast, and everyone would attend. Later on, when we wanted to make the girls' varsity team a big deal, we would have a kidnap breakfast where all the new girls who were going to be on the varsity team got kidnapped.

Life in high school was more than diving and football. Coach was very excited to get his driver's license.

It was suddenly cool to drive. There was a student parking lot and everything. But I couldn't drive unless I was able to pay for my own insurance. That's when I really went out and got a job.

Splish Splash

Prior to that, I'd been a box boy at a grocery store, and I worked at a car wash. Then I worked at two different gas stations, and when they graduated me to a dollar twenty-five an hour, I thought that life couldn't get any better.

Gas was twenty-two cents a gallon in those days. That was the time when big oil companies were trying to drive the independents out of business. They would just crash the gas price to a point that the independents couldn't survive. That's what gas wars were all about. When you stop and think about it, it was a very cruel thing.

Coach continued his football career at Long Beach City College. His positions stayed the same: offensive guard and defensive middle linebacker or noseguard. His team was a very good one. Their star player was known as the ghost of La Palma.

He'd gone to Anaheim High School, and his name was Mickey Flynn. He's famous in Orange County high school football lore. He got his nickname because Anaheim High School played their home games at La Palma Stadium. He was the "ghost" because nobody could tackle him. He was really good.

That was the season of 1957, and I think we had a ten and two season. We got a junior college bowl game that year that we won. It was the Alfalfa Bowl, and it was up on the high desert in Lancaster. We still had a fairly good team the next year in 1958, and that's when I got recruited to the University of Denver.

When Coach first went to Long Beach College, his emphasis was not on academics but football.

My career goal was to join the fire department. These days, you pretty much need a college education to get on the fire department. At that time, it wasn't necessary. My fallback plan was that I knew I could get sponsored into the longshoremen's union. If I didn't get on the fire department, two of my best friends were longshoremen, and I thought about joining them. So, at the onset of my college experience, my focus was athletics.

But then, Coach got very lucky. He worked with a man who is legendary in the Long Beach and US sports worlds, Monte Nitzkowski. Monte has a storied aquatics career. He swam and played water polo for the **UCLA Bruins in 1950 and 1951 and represented the United States in Helsinki, Finland, at the 1952 Olympic Games. He became one of the world's foremost authorities in water polo by coaching Long Beach City College to thirty-two conference water polo championships and twelve conference swim titles during 1954 to 1989. Nitzkowski acted as the US water polo assistant coach at the 1968 Olympics and was appointed head coach for the 1972, 1980, and 1984 games.**

As a diver, our team would either practice before or after swim workout. I started fooling around helping Monte Nitzkowski take timing splits. I started helping him with the swim workouts. That's where my interest in coaching started. On numerous occasions, he would say to me, "You should think about coaching; you would be good. You should think about a coaching career."

Other individuals whom Tom counts as mentors include Tom Murphy, his coach at University of Denver; Al Irwin, Orange Coast College swim coach; and Chuck Bittick, former world record holder in the backstroke and an NCAA champion.

Nine

University of Denver

Another important mentor entered Coach's life when he began studying at the University of Denver (DU). When Coach arrived at the University of Denver in 1959, he was already focused on becoming a coach. The dean of the men's physical education department at Denver was a man aptly named Dean Richardson.

> We had a fairly small department—no more than fifteen or twenty students—and that was great because the dean spent a lot of time counseling us and teaching us coaching theory. I really valued that time. The men's physical education department might have been one of the smaller departments on campus, so we got one-on-one time with the dean that we might not have gotten elsewhere.

Coach was offered a full-ride football scholarship to the University of Denver. Unbeknownst to him, his football days were numbered. In his second year at Denver, the football program was canceled. Chancellor Chester Allen made the call. He wanted to direct the sports money toward improving DU academics. He said that football was operating in the red, and he observed that the student body had become more interested in ice hockey than in football. The team's last game was on Thanksgiving Day, November 24, 1960. They defeated Colorado State twenty-one to twelve.

The university generously honored all its football scholarship commitments. But many of the DU players decided to transfer to other universities with football programs. Coach transferred his scholarship to the DU diving program. He had dived as a walk-on during his first year at Denver. For the rest of his career there, he dove on scholarship—a football scholarship.

> If a program is dropped from a school, then any athlete in that program is immediately eligible to play for another school. They don't have to sit on the bench or have any other transfer penalty. So, many of the guys on the team did transfer. Many went to the University of Tulsa.
>
> But those guys could definitely have stayed at Denver on scholarship. They could have gotten fat and not had to do a thing! It was a great thing that Denver did for those of us affected by their decision to drop football—it was a classy thing that they did. To this day, the University

of Denver is a very expensive school. And they were willing to honor all the scholarships they'd given—up to four years of scholarship money—for athletes coming on board as freshmen.

The swimming coach at Denver was a man named Tom Murphy. He was from Brooklyn and brought chutzpah to his program in Denver. Coach remembers that he would always finagle new station wagons from local car dealers to transport the team to meets all over the central and southwest states.

We had meets in Salt Lake City, Provo, Utah, Albuquerque, New Mexico, and Ames, Iowa. We traveled into Texas and Wyoming. Coach would always get three brand-new station wagons, and we traveled in them. We didn't have a huge team, about fifteen or sixteen guys—we certainly weren't the DU hockey team. But there we were, traveling in brand-new station wagons. Coach Murphy was a funny guy. He had really good rapport with everyone on the team and out in the community, too.

The DU diving coach was Jim Hartman. He was a high school coach in Denver who also coached the college team. Coach and he became very good friends. Eventually, Coach would do his student teaching at Jim Hartman's high school.

Tom Murphy and Jim Hartman were delighted to have Coach on their team on his unexpected scholarship. His Long Beach College team had been California state champions for two years running. Coach had finished second in the California State Championship in 1958 and was named to the Junior College All American team that year. During his two years diving at Denver, Coach placed in the top three in the Skyline Conference both years. He faced stiff competition from very good divers at the University of New Mexico and the University of Utah.

When I first got involved with diving at Denver, there was one senior with a real diving scholarship. I dove with him one year. His name was Gary Latrelle, and he was on a full ride. His uncle was in charge of the university security department. Gary got us some really cool jobs, and that was back in a time before the NCAA started cracking down on college jobs. Our premier athletes at the University of Denver were the hockey players. They were NCAA champions two of the three years I was at Denver. Our ski team had two Norwegians who skied from Norway in the 1960 Olympics in Squaw Valley. Those guys had the best jobs on campus—but, saying that, I don't think any job was cooler than the one I had in 1960.

On campus, there is a facility called DRI, which stands for the Denver Research Institute. You had to have a level-one government security clearance to enter that facility. My job was to go into the facility and literally walk the length of an ordinary home kitchen. There was a panel there that I had to open up and switch on some lights. I would open the panel, switch on the lights, close the panel, walk ten or fifteen feet to the door, and leave the building. To get my government clearance, I had to have an FBI background check. The Feds showed up at my mother's house in Southern California. As the story goes, it scared the devil out of my mother. She had no clue. "What the heck has he done now?" she wondered. And this was all so I could have the key to an insignificant room in an insignificant building in the Denver Research Institute. So, that was pretty cool; I had a lot of fun with that story.

Splish Splash

The next job Latrelle helped Coach land was as an ambulance attendant for the school infirmary. At all DU home hockey games, Coach was one of the guys who manned the ambulance.

> For the job, I had to take a Red Cross training course that prepared us to administer first aid and to respond to trauma and bleeding—that type of thing. Hockey players are very susceptible to injury, and this was before helmets were required. They would—all the time—get facial cuts from the puck as well as their teeth knocked out. A hockey player would smile at you, and it was just an empty void. Tough, oh my gosh, were those guys tough! Anyway, at the games, the guy who drove the Zamboni, the ice-cleaning machine, would pull out from the ice, and we would back the ambulance in. We would sit in the back of the ambulance right at the centerline and watch all the home hockey games.

It was a historic time to have centerline seats at DU hockey games.

> This was the national championship team. Not only that, we were very proud of our five wins and two ties against Olympic teams on their way to Squaw Valley in 1960. We beat the United States and tied them in a two-game series—and they won the gold medal that year. We tied the USSR, we beat Norway, and we beat Sweden. After that, the University of Denver proclaimed themselves the "Unofficial 1960 Olympic Champions"!

In his fifth year (1961–1962) at Denver, Coach's eligibility was gone. In those days, the practice of red shirting was not much used. So, the typical college scholarship expired in four years. Nowadays, many athletes will practice but not compete in their freshmen year.

> You might remember that when I was at Long Beach City College, my career goal had been to join the fire department. So, while I was there, I took some classes that, although not under water basket weaving, were not courses that transferred for credit at the University of Denver. I had to do a fifth year to make up for those courses.
> In that year, I needed to complete my student teaching requirement and a couple of other education theory courses. So, I didn't have a heavy academic load, and I had time to be student assistant to the swimming coach, Tom Murphy. I coached diving and helped him with swimming. That was where I got my first real grounding in coaching.

One day, a teenage kid was at the pool, watching Coach with his divers. The kid's name was Bernie Wrightson. He wanted to be a diver—a good diver. Bernie's dad was an airline pilot, and he hired Coach to work with Bernie.

> I coached Bernie for the better part of a year. I didn't immediately know how successful a diver he would turn out to be, but I knew instantly that he was very, very talented. He'd been a gymnast, which gave him the build and the aptitude for diving.
> Many of the most successful high school divers are ex-gymnasts. When you do really high, high diving, you almost always do feetfirst entries. That's a real advantage for gymnasts because

with all their tricks, they land on their feet—you don't land on your head. I have always jokingly said that a true diver is too smart to do that! You have to be a dumb gymnast to do all the things that they do and then go into the water feetfirst. Bernie will concur with that.

I remember I was teaching Bernie to learn a "list," which is the vernacular for the dives that you do. He was eager to learn and had a lot of natural ability. He had a gift, and that gift really paid off for him. Bernie would come in and dive with the University of Denver team, and then his dad was paying me a little extra to work one-on-one with him, too.

I remember once when I was trying to get him to do a two and a half reverse, which is a dive you have to be called out of. It's completely blind. I had sent away for a diving suit for him—made by Mabs. I told Bernie that if he did a two and a half reverse, then I would get him a Mabs diving suit. So, that was his motivation to learn that dive. He did, and I got him the suit.

You absolutely have to have a lot of trust in your coach to allow him to call you out of a blind dive. From the coach's perspective, the way you teach a diver to react to a call is by having the diver start with just a single summersault. When you call, the diver pops and does a feetfirst entry from a front flip. Then you work up to a one and a half, then a double, and then a two and a half. A two and a half was as far as Bernie went at that age while I was coaching him. Later, he went on to do a three and half. Now, divers do a four and a half forward, three and a half inward—two and a half reverses. They are doing some phenomenal things. So, you have to learn to trust your coach to properly call you out of a dive. Another word for that would be courage. It takes a lot of courage.

Bernie was with us diving at the Air Force Academy. They had a beautiful, brand-new facility—indoor, ten-meter tower—with really top of the line diving boards. He met Dick Smith there, who was the diving coach at Arizona State University in Phoenix. Dick Smith gave Bernie a full-ride scholarship to ASU, and he dove for them. That's where he really took off as a diver.

He became NCAA champion, National AAU champion, and in 1968, made the Olympic team. He won the gold in three-meter springboard diving there. From there, he became national champion several times. Another feather in his cap is that he was the first diver to win one meter, three meter, and ten meter at the same national championship meet. Triple national champion. In his time, he was regarded as the finest diver in the world. So, that was fun for me to have been just a little part of his success.

At a recent party at Mark Hastings's house in Palm Springs, Mark had a picture that was taken of him and Bernie when Mark was twelve years old. He had the picture enlarged and displayed at the party. Bernie was just blown away when he saw that picture with Mark—which he did not remember. The picture was taken when Bernie was at the Olympic trials, so obviously, his mind was in a very focused place.

At the party, I told Bernie, "You don't realize it, but you have been a part of this family forever. That picture has not only been a motivator for Mark but also an inspiration that he has shared with all four of his kids, his friends, his relatives, and on and on." That's when I took Bernie away from the displayed picture and showed him the framed one hanging in Mark's hall. He just stared and said, "Oh my gosh!"

I said, "Isn't it amazing that you can have so much influence on somebody—and that you have absolutely no knowledge of it?"

Ten

Love and Marriage

The most significant experience Coach De Long was to have at Denver did not happen at either Hilltop Stadium or the DU aquatics facility. It happened when he got hooked up on a blind date with a cute coed from Cañon City, Colorado.

Coach was living with a group of Denver swimmers (many of them from California) in a house located about a block from campus. The house had been a doctor's office, so the rooms were unusual because they all included a counter and sink. The students all pitched in to pay the rent, which Coach remembers to be about seventeen dollars a month. Canadian swimmer Jack Kelso, University of Denver's first NCAA champion, lived at the house with Coach. Later, Jack would be best man at Coach's wedding. The house was a hangout spot for all the swimmers on the team.

Pat Wilson frequently visited the house. He was a former swimmer who attended all the meets. Pat was teaching physical education in Lakewood, a Denver suburb. He taught at what was called a cottage school—a small facility with only two grades at each site. Lakewood was growing, and as it grew, the plan was to turn each cottage school into a regular elementary school. Clara Darnell taught at a cottage school in Lakewood, too. As Coach recalls, "One day, Pat Wilson said to me, 'I know this cute little gal, and you guys would be a perfect fit!'"

It was Christmastime, and Coach was to go back to California for the holidays. It was the end of January before he first called Clara. The two eventually agreed to meet. It might have been the classic blind date, except even then, Clara had some surprises up her sleeve.

It wasn't easy. I first asked her if she'd like to go out on a Friday night, and she said she had plans. I said, "What about Saturday?" And she said, "I have plans." So, I thought, after two strikes, do you go for the third, or do you take a hint? "What about Sunday?"

She invited me over to her apartment. So, I'm thinking, "Whoa. She's inviting me to her apartment."

What she said was that if I didn't think she was presentable, then I didn't have to go out with her, and if I wasn't what she hoped, then she wouldn't have to go out with me.

I knocked on the door, and she answered it. And guess what? She had her roommate and her roommate's boyfriend there with her!

The two hit it off well, and very shortly thereafter, they were going out without a chaperone.

> I had my little Austin-Healey Sprite. I will never forget it. It was about ten degrees, and we're on our way out to dinner and a movie. The back glass window in the soft top had broken. I had replaced it myself and fastened it with these tiny little snaps. We're driving down the street, and the back window collapsed. It was absolutely freezing cold.
>
> The movie was *Pillow Talk* with Doris Day and Rock Hudson. That was what we saw on our first date.

It was the winter of 1962. Coach was doing his student teaching, and Clara was teaching first grade. They were together every day for two months straight. Coach was to graduate in the spring. His mom and his sister came back to Denver for the graduation. Neither was pleased with the budding romance.

> They told me I didn't have any business being involved with anybody, that I had bills to pay for school.
>
> Well, anyway, we broke up. And I learned later that I broke Clara's heart. She stayed in Denver, and I came back to Long Beach, where I was a lifeguard that summer.

Clara was friends with a diving pal of Coach's. He also was from California and was engaged to a woman from Denver. Clara was in their wedding, which took place in the summer of 1962 in Denver.

> In the fall of that year, my friend called Clara and asked her if she'd ever want to talk to me. She said, "Oh yeah, sure." So, one thing led to another, and we got back together. We saw each other when she came to California at Christmas when she and her mother visited Clara's sister, Norma, who was living in Santa Monica. Then we saw each other again over Easter vacation. That's when I gave her a ring, and we became engaged.
>
> The two months we dated in Denver was really the only long stretch of time we spent together. We spent four or five days during Christmas in Long Beach. Then we spent four or five days during Easter week when we got engaged. The next time I saw her was when I drove back to Cañon City, Colorado, for the wedding in June. It was just meant to be.

Coach recalls that they kept in touch during their times apart using tape recordings and by writing to each other every day. Phone calls were prohibitively expensive in those days, so the two did not speak frequently.

Coach rented an apartment in Costa Mesa for the couple. He laughs that it cost $112 a month with maid service. He and Clara's brother-in-law, Paul Merhoff, drove back to Cañon City for the wedding. Clara's sister, Norma, had flown back earlier because she and Paul's son, Kurt, were going to be in the wedding.

Tom and Clara were married in 1963. He was still lifeguarding at the time and working on earning his California teaching credential.

Splish Splash

Our honeymoon was a trip back from Colorado. We drove from Cañon City, Colorado, via Las Vegas to Long Beach. We met up with my sister and brother-in-law in Las Vegas. I had gotten ten days off from the beach, from lifeguarding. We spent two nights getting to Las Vegas and maybe three nights in Las Vegas. It wasn't much of a honeymoon, especially compared to what happens these days. Still, something must have worked; we've been married over fifty years!

Tom and Clara had similar childhoods.

Our backgrounds were not that much different in many respects. Her dad homesteaded in eastern Colorado. I think he got fifty acres or something like that. He started raising cattle and crops. Clara has always said that they bought very little from the store; they grew almost everything. The only thing they bought from the store was flour and sugar.

Theirs was just the most barren, windy land you can imagine. In wintertime, it gets very cold. It's located about thirty-five miles east of Pueblo. If you drive west from Pueblo for about twenty minutes, then you start winding up into the Rocky Mountains, but Clara's family lived in the opposite direction. Their land is a little rolling, but it's mostly flat.

Both of us grew up to become very self-sufficient. You have to be creative in that kind of environment. I know that I spent hours and hours and hours just being creative—as Clara did, too. We were on our own a lot—sometimes with friends—but you learned to occupy a whole day doing lots of different things.

There were lots of similarities in the ways Clara and I grew up. But I always get to brag that I grew up poorer than she did!

Clara's dad had homesteaded in eastern Colorado and was a rancher. They didn't like the schools where they'd homesteaded, and they wanted something different for Clara and her sister. That's when they sold some of his property, and they bought a motel in Cañon City. It was called the Latchstring Motel. Her dad owned another motel after that. He didn't manage it; he hired someone to run it.

Turns out the motel business is on both sides of the family!

Clara's dad did a lot of land swapping and trading. He loaned money. He would go down to the veterans' hall, drink coffee, and loan money. He kept a small spiral notebook in his shirt pocket in which he wrote all his loan notes: "Glenn borrowed X dollars at X percent and the payback is…" He would keep every payback in that notebook. As the money was paid, he would scratch it off in the book.

We have his old desk. When we got it, we found all kinds of old checks he had written in 1919 and 1920: two head of cattle, fifteen dollars. They are keepsakes and a real look at life during those days.

Tom De Long with Sharon Hastings

Coach and Clara's wedding day, June 22, 1963

Eleven

Clown Diving

Coach began his clown-diving career while he was at Long Beach Poly. In those days, clown diving was quite popular. The clowns came out to dive between acts in all the water shows. Their acts allowed costume and set changes in the water extravaganza shows that were then very popular. When Coach was at Long Beach Poly, the female athletes didn't swim competitively; instead, they did water ballet.

> Our clown diving was associated with their show. It was a big event that ran for several evenings, and all the parents would come to watch. The girls would spend all semester preparing for this one extravaganza.
>
> There were a couple of really famous divers—Hobie Billingsley comes to mind—who were fantastic clown divers. It took a certain amount of courage, a certain amount of skill, and a certain amount of craziness to clown dive and be effective.

Coach and his pals Eric Kossi and Don Shsorsky formed the clown-diving team. They were so skilled and funny that word spread about their act. In Coach's junior and senior years, the trio did six shows a year, performing at Long Beach Poly, Long Beach Wilson, and Jordan High schools.

> We never got paid for our performances; it was just so much fun to do. We got to see all those cute girls in their swimsuits; that was pretty good pay.
>
> Later on, after clown diving at Poly, I settled into a partnership with Bill Underwood. We worked together after I got to Long Beach City College. He was diving at Orange Coast College. He and I did several shows a year.
>
> When I was back at the University of Denver, Bill and I did a big show there when they opened the Celebrity Center. The place had an eighty-lane bowling alley and a fifty-meter pool—a skating rink—it was a big complex that the Disney Company built. We did a clown-diving show at the inauguration of the swimming pool there.

Bill and I decided to do the act professionally for a couple of summers, from 1963 to 1965. We did shows at country clubs and places like that. In 1968, we did a show when they opened Belmont Plaza in Long Beach. By that time, Mark and Mike Hastings had become my partners. Probably the last show we did was one of the ones I did for Shirley Kelly's water show at Foothill.

Twelve

Lifeguarding

Once Coach and his family moved to Long Beach in the 1950s, the beach became a big part of his life. Beyond the surf and the pretty girls, the young men who kept the water safe for swimmers—the lifeguards—fascinated Coach.

I would watch them when I first started going to the beach as a little kid. There were several lifeguards then who were very good—in fact, there were some All American football players. Johnny Olszewski was a Long Beach boy who played at St. Anthony's High School, went on to be an All American at Cal, and then played professional football. Scrappy Ray was also a professional football player. George Timberlake, who was an All American at USC, was there at that time.

I remember as a little junior high kid just being in complete awe of those guys. They were gods to me, fast and giant. They would run wind sprints on the hard sand down by the water. There were always four or five of them. I'd hang out with a couple of guys down at the beach, and we would go and watch the lifeguards.

Tom began his own ten-year lifeguarding career at age eighteen, becoming one of the guards he had so admired as a child. In those days, there were two beaches at Long Beach, West Beach and East Beach. West Beach was the place where many families from Compton and Watts would come to swim and play. Often, those inner-city kids were unskilled swimmers.

For the most part, the kids were horrible swimmers. Probably not a lot of time in the water. If those kids were off the bottom, then they were in trouble. So, you had to be a hawk, just a hawk, in watching them. There was no surf on the beach because of the breakwater. The Los Angeles River comes down there, so holes would develop on the bottom. You could be waist deep in water, and the next step, you're up over your head. So, we had to really work.

I think those days at West Beach made me realize that lifeguarding was serious stuff. I mean, you have this idea that if you're a lifeguard, then you're tan and you've got a good body and all the babes are watching you. But you learn. And our chief was a taskmaster in that regard. So, at age eighteen, I first realized that I had responsibility for people—sometimes in life-or-death situations.

Coach remembers some special privileges that came from his days guarding at West Beach.

> Those families from Watts would come to the beach for the day, and they would bring a spread that you would not believe. They befriended the lifeguards because of the way we were watching out for their babies. So, they brought along these huge picnics, and they would feed us. We ate good, let me tell you!

Coach met his lifelong friend Fred Simpson while they were both in high school. Fred was a swimmer, and Coach was a diver on the Long Beach Poly High team. They became great friends—and competitors.

> Fred Simpson and I often shared the same lifeguard shift—either that, or we were an hour apart. Shifts weren't awarded by seniority. If he could, then the captain would pretty much give you the shift that you wanted. My favorite shifts were eleven to seven p.m. or noon to eight p.m. It was never boring then—lots of things happening.

A long-standing tradition among Long Beach lifeguards is the Lifeguard Beach Olympics. Coach has many fond memories of those competitions.

> Pretty soon, I was competing in the Lifeguard Beach Olympics I had watched when I was a kid. We had several different events. Some were pretty ordinary like sprinting the fifty-yard dash. We did hop, step, and jump competitions. We had triple jump—leap, leap, leap—three leaps with a two-foot landing. This was Fred Simpson's favorite event. He says I never beat him—but I think I did at least a couple of times. The event occurred on the berm where the sand drops down. You get a nice place up on the top, and then you bend your knees, swing your arms, and jump down backward as far as you can. We got quite good at this.
> On a normal morning, we'd have three or four regular guys competing. Sometimes we might have guys who would be stationed at our beach for one or two days—guys who did rotations and filled in on different guys' days off.
> Early in the morning before the morning overcast burned off, it would be pretty cold. There would be zero people on the beach—as in nobody. The captain liked us doing these competitions because we were being physically active.
> We were pretty loose about our events. If a big piece of driftwood came in overnight, then we would have a contest throwing it for distance. The big football types always beat the little skinny swim types in that event.
> Very, very early when skim boards were just coming out—we all had skim boards—we'd go for distance and do tricks. You could hook your hand in the sand and that would start you spinning. Then you would see how many times you could spin around. I remember I always used to get sand between my legs, and I would just get raw. Like sandpaper between my legs.

Splish Splash

Another great lifeguard competition involves the long surfboats called dories. Coach recalls some favorite stories.

I got involved with dory racing while I was lifeguarding. This was before the dories from Australia—the self-bailing dories—arrived on the scene. We used the old, heavy wooden dories when we were racing. The way the Australian dories are built is that they have a false bottom in them. The false bottom is an airlock. They can't sink; they can swamp and tip over. Then they have scuppers, which are drains. So, if you take on water, the water just drains out of them. Boy, the difference is dramatic—from the boats we raced to the Australian ones—to now the ones they race that are made of fiberglass.

Fast-forward a half a century—soon after we started our Long Beach Lifeguard Alumni Association. We were getting ready to celebrate the centennial of Long Beach lifeguards. The program started in 1906, so this was 2006. Our group came up with the idea of starting a program called the Fellowship of the Dory.

Thirty guys committed to paying for a dory they had constructed back east at Lowell's Boat Shop in Amesbury, Massachusetts. It's the oldest operating boat shop in America. Everyone who participated got a wooden plaque. The dory they had made is custom, and it's really beautiful. It's all natural wood with brass oarlocks; it's really, really nice. The plan is that any lifeguard who so desires can be buried at sea. His or her ashes will be spread from the dory. There's a plaque in the dory with everybody's name on it who is a member of the Fellowship of the Dory. I have always said I want to be cremated and buried at sea. I jokingly say that way I can spend eternity being in every kid's sandcastle!

So, lifeguarding taught me a lot. Life is about having fun, but it is also serious—with serious consequences. And lifeguarding also put a time regimen into my life. Now, you're really responsible to a schedule.

Coach in Long Beach

Tom De Long with Sharon Hastings

Long Beach Poly Diving Team
Coach is second from bottom

Long Beach City 1958 College Football Team
Coach (#62) 1st row, third from the left

Splish Splash

Coach and friends at the University of Denver

Mark Hasings, Bernie Wrightson at the 1968 Olympic Trials

Tom De Long with Sharon Hastings

1965 Long Beach Lifeguards

Thirteen

Coaching

In 1964, Coach was a substitute teacher at thirteen different high schools. He counts that year as a blessing, as it gave him the opportunity to sample several schools and to teach under many athletics directors and coaches. Although he didn't understand it at the time, he used that year to "shop" for the kind of high school teaching and coaching situation that would best suit him.

Even though he subbed in three different schools in Garden Grove—and was eventually offered a coaching position at one of them—Coach never felt comfortable in that district. He remembers their pay scale at the time was the highest of the districts he considered, but something told him to look elsewhere.

> I did a long-term sub at Corona del Mar High School. But the aquatics coach, Ted Newland, seemed entrenched. It was a dream job—but he wasn't leaving. Ironically, he wasn't as rooted at Corona del Mar as it seemed to me then. Turns out, he coached much of his career at UCI [University of California, Irvine], where he won a couple of NCAA championships. He was appointed an Olympic coach as well.

But Coach knew none of that in 1964. Still, the time at Corona del Mar was useful. He recognized many of the attractive qualities of that school at Foothill High.

Another high school where Coach felt "at home" was Newport Harbor High School.

> They were offering me the coaching job at Newport Harbor High School. I also had another job offer at a Garden Grove high school,—Balsa Grande. But after I met Bob Osborne and Jerry Sedoo at Foothill, I came home and told Clara, "There's this really cool little school out in the middle of some orange groves. At Foothill, we're going to get a brand-new swimming pool. And I am going to be able to start my own program." Newport had always had a good aquatics program—a real swimming tradition. But I decided at the last minute I wouldn't take the job there. I accepted the job at Foothill and let the other ones go. And I have never once regretted it.

Tom De Long with Sharon Hastings

The coach who originally took the job at Newport Harbor was there only two seasons. Then Bill Barnett got the job. An Orange County legend, Bill Barnett coached at Newport Harbor for forty-nine years. Coach and he competed against each other for over thirty years.

The Foothill High School pool was a labor of love for Coach. He and Bill Furniss headed the committee that designed the facility. At that time, pools were generally designed in an L shape. One lifeguard could watch both the deep and the shallow ends. The trouble with L-shaped pools is that they allowed fewer racing lanes The Foothill pool was the first pool in Orange County designed to be twenty-five yards by twenty-five meters. This allowed for ten racing lanes. After the Foothill pool was built in 1967, other high schools adopted this pool design.

Coach describes himself as "a kid waiting for Christmas" while the pool was under construction. He slipped out at every opportunity to check on its progress. Sometimes when he found no construction workers on-site, he felt deep frustration. Finally, in the spring of 1967, the pool was completed. Coach said, "I think I felt complete ownership of that pool. It was my pool."

Coach remembers innumerable quick trips in from Costa Mesa to deal with the pilot light on the original pool heater. Any lucky gust of wind would put it out. Santa Ana winds were a particular plague.

I can remember driving from Costa Mesa to Foothill—thirteen miles—on a Sunday evening at eight or nine o'clock at night to make sure that the pilot light hadn't gone out—because I didn't want to cancel Monday morning workout because the pool was too cold. Any time we had a Santa Ana wind, I was always going up to Foothill to check the pilot light. One of the happiest days of my life was when we finally installed electronic ignition.

There are lots of stories about Coach's "ownership" of that pool. Here is one of his favorites.

They'd built a cinder block wall around the pool. And when the pool was first built, we had very limited space for people to sit. Down on the football field were several sets of bleachers that lined one whole side of the track. Three sets went past the end zone. One day, I told the kids that I wanted everyone to bring a crescent wrench to Saturday practice. So, come Saturday, I had all the kids—there must have been fifteen of us—go down to the football field, and we dismantled one set of bleachers and carried it up through the double gates going into the pool. Then we reassembled it on the pool deck. It was a lot of work. Don Hand was the dad of two of my swimmers, and he worked for the Southern California Edison Company. One of the Hand boys helped with the bleachers that Saturday. Afterward, he told me he was going to tell his dad about what we had done; he thought his dad might be able to help.

So, Don and I had a little talk, and the next Saturday, he showed up with a company truck. It was the kind of truck that Southern California Edison uses to lift telephone poles. I got a key to the big gate on Dodge Avenue, and we took the truck down to the football field. We dragged the remaining two sets of bleachers up the driveway, and then Mr. Hand hooked up a cable, lifted the bleachers, swung them over the brand-new pool wall, and set them down on the pool deck.

Splish Splash

> Those were the bleachers we had all the time at the Foothill pool. I stole them from the football field. Jerry Sedoo was hopping mad because he wanted those for his baseball field. Well, I got to keep them because, without the SC Edison truck, there was no way to move them!
>
> I cannot even imagine something like that happening these days. Even then, I was thinking that if they had dropped the bleachers on the new wall, then that probably would have ended my coaching career at Foothill.

Later in Coach's career, he would often be asked to speak at coaching clinics. One piece of advice he always gave came from his love for and ownership of his pool.

> A thing I would always advise at those clinics was to take care of your pool man. Although he's often "just" a custodian, he may be the most important person you deal with because he can shut you out of workout in a heartbeat. I always took care of my pool man. I made sure to get him a Christmas present. I tried to make him understand he was a very important part of the program. We would make him an honorary letter winner—those kinds of things. Ralph Teeter was my first pool man at Foothill. My kids and I were always respectful of him.

But we're getting ahead of the Foothill High School swimming story. When Coach first came to Foothill, he had no pool. No pool meant no fall water polo. He was asked to coach the wrestling team.

> My first coaching assignment at Foothill was in the winter, and it was the wrestling team. There are three sport seasons, and wrestling is after football in the fall. I had a lot of football players who wrestled because it was just a natural for them to do that. I had a great time being the wrestling coach. I had wrestled as a kid at the YMCA, and I took the Foothill program knowing that it would be just for one year.

Claude Wiseman, a chemistry teacher at Foothill, and Al Marzelli, a future Foothill principal, took over the wrestling program after Coach went on to coach aquatic sports.

Fourteen

THE EARLY YEARS AT FOOTHILL

In the fall of 1965, Coach called a meeting for Foothill kids interested in swimming. It was then that he met the guys on his first team: Ron Anderson, Jeff Aaron, Bill Canham, Tom Courtney, Tom Drummund, Chip Furniss, Ted Hall, Len Hollowell, Stephan Lang, Bob Bannon, Woody Haig, Tony Ilo, John Lenz, Chuck Lockwood, Dan Prigmore, Dale Summerl, Dan Summerl, and Richard Whitinaw.

> I came home and told Clara, "I've really lucked out; I have a nest of swimmers at Foothill, and I didn't even know it." I literally had no idea. I had done no research before taking the job. Nobody would do that now.

One of the things Coach did that first year was write a Foothill Swim Team welcome letter.

> The challenge will be great, but the rewards will be much greater. 1966 will be a year for setting traditions for every swimmer who follows this first team.
> Repeat to yourself each day: what I am to be, I am now becoming.
> Our program is going to be a stiff assignment. It will take a boy with real "stuff" to even try it out. A weakling will not even try to tackle it.
> This is the challenge from your coach. Our goal from the start will be to place Foothill High School on the Southern California swimming map.

Coach remembers when he invited his lifelong friend Chuck Bittick to his first swim team. Chuck was an All American swimmer at USC—and a many-time national champion. He was the world record holder in the two-hundred-meter backstroke and the first athlete to make the Olympic team in two sports—swimming and water polo in the 1960 Olympics in Rome. The schedule did not permit Chuck to compete in both sports, so he chose water polo. Coach and Chuck were teammates at Long Beach City College, where they won the California State Junior College Championship in 1958.

> Chuck came and talked to the kids, and he was a real source of inspiration for them. Here's an Olympian, and we're just starting our program from scratch. I remember the kids were just in awe of an Olympian. That was cool.

Splish Splash

From the very beginning, Coach was aware of his larger purpose in coaching swimming.

> One thing I've always believed in and taught is that the lessons learned in competitive swimming have a tremendous carryover into later life. The sacrifices that you have to make to be a competitive swimmer mean that when you get into college, you'll have the discipline to succeed. Your roommates or your fraternity brothers may say, "Forget that test. Let's go out and party." The swimmer knows from his experience that he can't do that. And It's not that tough to make that choice because he's used to making those kinds of sacrifices. He knows how to get up at five thirty in the morning to go to workout, or to give up Easter vacation for swim workout, or to do double workouts in the summer when everyone else is going to the beach—the swimmer has lots of practice doing those things. That lesson was one of the good things I was able to preach to my swimmers over my whole career.
>
> It's amazing the success kids on Foothill's swim teams have achieved. We used to have an alumni water polo game every year. The last time I coached the alumni group, I started six medical doctors and one attorney. These kids go on and on and on with a high level of success. But I think that swimming is a sport that attracts successful people. It's a sport where you spend many hours by yourself swimming back and forth in a pool. You have to know about perseverance to succeed—and in the end, perseverance is the marker of most success.

While the Foothill pool was under construction, the Foothill High School swim team worked out in Orange, California, at the Sammy Lee Three Cs Swim School. The Three Cs stood for Caldwell, Caldwell, and Caldwell—the Caldwell family had originally owned the facility. Coach and his swimmers bussed to the facility after school, and he remembers that at least once a week, the bus driver was late to pick them up.

> We swam from four thirty to six p.m. It was winter, and it was cold and often windy—miserable because Three Cs was an outdoor pool. I can remember all of us going into the filter room and hunkering down in there around the heater to stay warm. Across the street was one of the first time and temperature displays in our area. When the temperature dipped under sixty degrees—into the fifties—I would take notice during the workout. It would be really, really cold as the kids got out of the pool—and dark. It seemed like those were always the days when the bus would be late to pick us up. There were numerous times I had to call and find out where the bus was. Then parents started to get on the school district, complaining that their kids needed to get home to have dinner and study. After that, the situation got fixed, but we spent a lot of time in the filter room that fall.

Despite the challenges of the team's early busing experience at Foothill, Coach was a firm believer in having his kids travel on the bus to swim meets together. He remembers that swimmers and their parents often asked for exceptions, but unless it was something like an SAT test early on a Saturday morning—after a late Friday night meet—he held firm.

> I was unusual in this policy. There were many schools that didn't even use bus transportation—they carpooled to meets. I just felt it was important—and I have had enough feedback through

the years to know that practice was meaningful to the kids. It underlined that they were part of a team. Singing and having a good time on the bus provided my swimmers with some of their fondest memories.

    Coach maintained certain rituals for the bus. The varsity got to get on the bus first and to pick the seats they wanted, then the JVs, and then the other swimmers. I'd hear comments like, "I'm never going to get to pick my seat." "Why not?" "Because I'll never make varsity."

Over the many years that Coach presided over Foothill High School aquatics, there were many great meets and rivalries. Of them all, Coach enjoyed the continuing competition with Long Beach Wilson best. He remembers fondly the beginning of the Foothill/Long Beach Wilson swimming rivalry that continues to this day.

I'd always competed against Wilson when I was at Poly. I wanted them on our schedule because they were good; they always won their league. I tried to schedule all our nonleague meets against the very best teams. I didn't want to swim against anybody we could easily beat. I wanted our kids to swim up against the best competition we could find.

    We first beat Long Beach Wilson one night in the early seventies. Tim Shaw was swimming for Wilson; he later became a world record holder. We had to break the CIF freestyle relay record—in a dual meet—to win that meet, which we did. Over the years, we had some really good competitions with Long Beach Wilson. Those have always been some of my favorite swim meets.

Fifteen

Coaching Strategies

When Coach was first at Foothill, he created the Under a Minute Club. Any swimmer who broke a minute in the one hundred freestyle belonged to the club. Later, he took a page from Peter Daland's coaching book at USC and started keeping a top fifty list for each stroke. Coach remembers that Foothill was one of the first high school programs to do so.

> We kept a book for each season in which we would list our top fifty swimmers. We would score each place—fifty points if you are first; one point if you are fiftieth. Then we would add up each swimmer's points. When I retired from coaching in 1993, the female swimmer Megan Logan, who was the all-time highest scorer in swimming during all these years later, was still number two on the list.
>
> That list was a great motivator for my kids. They would just be so excited to even make the list. All the kids on the team knew what it took to get on the list—to make fiftieth.
>
> Lou Dean was the person who kept up with all the data when she was working at Foothill. She had a spreadsheet on her computer, and she would punch in the numbers. It was so cool. She ran the student bookstore at Foothill; her son was a swimmer.

Coach played another motivating game with his swimmers. He called it the swat rule. Before early-morning workouts, the kids, understandably, lingered in the warm locker room. It was hard to head out into the cold and then to dive into a chilly pool.

> I would just open the door—as I'm coming out of the coaches' office—and I would yell, "Swat rule!" It was like someone flipped on a light, and there were a thousand scurrying cockroaches! They just ran into the pool. In they would go, and I would watch for the last one to hit the water.
>
> Whoever was last had to come out and grab hold of starting block number five. Then I would take a kickboard and hang a swat on his rear end. He would dive over the starting block into the water, and all the guys would say, "Don't rub it, don't rub it!" Finally, it got to a point that the kids figured out it stung much more to get a swat on a wet swimsuit than on a dry one.

So, the kid who knew he was going to be last would never go into the water. He would just run down to starting block number five and take his punishment.

Another practice, called "Pride", is a fond memory for Coach. Pride happened at the end of workout.

We would do sprints, and the last person to touch had to get out of the pool. It was amazing how much the kids hated to get out. You'd think they'd welcome having workout over. But no, the kids fought to stay in the pool. Usually, the game would go on until we got our winner—a good twelve to fifteen sprints down the pool. I would always try to end the game so that the last sprint would be down by the boys' locker room. As for the winner, he got a couple of jelly beans. Ultimately, there was an article in the paper about our pride games. The upshot of the article was that I sure got a lot of mileage out of a bag of jelly beans!

My top kids knew how to work the game. They would swim to the middle of the pack for the first sprints—making sure they weren't last—but they would save up for the final sprints. They knew that the top four or five guys at the end of the game were really going to have to work hard to not be eliminated. The kids who were out—instead of going into the locker room—they would stay in the water to see who the final few were going to be. Pride is one of my really fond memories.

Fun on the Foothill team was always a two-way street. Coach made a practice of always planning something special for April Fools' Day. Over time, however, the best pranks came from his swimmers.

A bunch of the guys snuck into the pool and switched all the starting blocks. They switched lane ten to the deep side and all the way across. When I came out that day, everyone was in their proper lanes. lane ten kids were in lane ten, but now it was on the deep side of the pool. And my top swimmers were in lane one.

My practice was to divide up the swimmers because there was a lot of goofing off among my less capable swimmers. I put my crazy kids in what they called the Alligator Lane—lane ten—where I could really watch them. Those were always the kids who were from forty to sixty percent serious—great kids, but I would have frustrated myself beyond recognition if I'd given them the same effort as I gave the top kids. I would have probably driven them all away.

So, there I am. "Ha-ha. Isn't this weird. Everybody switched lanes. April Fool. Oh boy, you really got me!" So, then I said, "Good joke. That's over."

"No," I heard back. "We're swimming in our proper lanes!" I looked and saw the lane number switches, and they really were in their proper lanes. So, I let them stay right where they were for that workout. Well, the lane ten kids just hated it. They were swimming in the deep end, and there was no bottom to stand on or push off of—or stop in the middle of a swim and walk awhile.

It really was a lot of work for the kids because they had to unbolt all the starting blocks and re-bolt them. Afterward, it was a lot of work for me—because I was the one who ended up having to put them all back together again!

Splish Splash

Peter Daland, the famed college coach at USC, had nicknames for his swimmers. It was a practice that Coach also employed.

> I did have a bunch of nicknames for my swimmers. JayBird was Jay Palchikoff, and Boney was Bob Bonebreak. Tina Summerl was TinaTuna. Bruce Furniss was B-Fur. His brother Chip was C-Fur. To this day, I still call Bruce B-Fur. Peter Daland, the swim coach at USC, was famous for shortening names so that he could write them down quickly. Maybe I got the habit from him. But we had a lot of fun nicknames over the years.

A saying that Coach always used was, "We never close."

> It was something that just evolved—because we literally never did close. Regardless of the weather, unless the pool was broken, we swam. Rain, shine, Santa Ana winds blowing whitecaps in the middle of the pool—we swam. One specific time I remember was in the middle of March—a rainy, miserable, cold day—probably in the low fifties with the wind blowing hard. Sixth-period athletics came along, and all the athletes start trickling into the locker room.
>
> The baseball coach goes over to the locker room door and yells, "Baseball. No practice today. Go home." Then the track coach comes to the door: "Track. No practice today. Go home." He was followed closely by the tennis coach, who stood at the door and shouted, "Tennis courts are wet. No practice today." Then here comes the golf coach: "No practice today."
>
> Finally, I head over to the door: "Swimming. Suit up!"
>
> It took a little persuasion from me for my swimmers to understand that was a positive thing—something really neat. The swim team never closed. When the going gets tough, we go right along as if nothing had happened. My kids got teased about having to swim in speedos and things like that. I am pretty sure they got their jabs back—because no one could ever call them wusses. After all, all those other athletes "closed and went home."
>
> The one little secret about that policy is that I was the one who was most miserable. The kids were in the pool, and the water was warm—much warmer than the air. I was the one out there getting buffeted around by the wind and rain. But it was worth it. I remember the kids got pretty creative. During rest intervals, they would pull the kickboards out and put them over their heads so they could avoid the cold rain pelting them.
>
> In the beginning when I would yell, "Suit up," there was some groaning and complaining. But I would never hide in the pool shed and coach from there. We were all in it together. I stayed out in the elements and took the pain because I knew they were in the same situation. That was a point of pride for me.
>
> I have always said that swimmers are made, not born. I had many kids who excelled—it was just the aura of the Foothill swim program. Success breeds success. Those kids achieved a lot more than if they had been a bigger fish in a different pool. A lot of my "little fish" did really, really well.

In the late 1960s and early 1970s, most of the successful high school swim programs were "fed" by successful age-group swimming programs. The Sammy Lee Swim School program famously "fed" some excellent swimmers into Lee Arth's renowned Fullerton High School program. Mission Viejo High School also benefited from the age-group swimming program that fed it. Coach De Long launched the Foothill Fins to provide the same benefit to his high school program.

> I had a whole bunch of kids running through all the age group levels. Rick LaRose was my assistant then. He went on to coach for a couple of seasons at Tustin High School. Then he got a really great job offer at the University of Arizona as the golf coach, where he's spent his whole career. The whole purpose of the Foothill Fins was to be a feeder program for the high school team.

Eventually, something had to give in Coach's life. The huge time commitment he made to his swimming, diving, and teaching responsibilities proved too much.

> I had to drop the Fins in 1971. It was just too time-consuming. A clincher was when I didn't see my children awake for twenty-six days in a row. I left in the morning before they got up, and I got home at night after they were in bed. I was coaching the Fins after I was coaching swim practice for the high school team. Then we had meets—either high school or age group—every weekend. I was away overnight on weekends, and I was leaving home early, early in the mornings to go to these swim meets. I finally said to myself, "This is crazy. I am spending my life with everybody else's kids and not my own." That's when I made the decision to give up the swim club and to just be the high school coach.

The Fins soon merged with the Placentia and Fullerton swim clubs. The merger was given the unlikely name of Fullplafoot! The team swam as Fullplafoot in the Orange County Swim Conference for two summers. Then they renamed the team SoCal. SoCal exits to this day as both a water polo and a swim club.

Sixteen

Foothill Girls' Swimming

Coach took over coaching the girls' swim team at Foothill in 1976. He ran the team coed with his boys' team from the onset. The varsity boys and girls worked out together.

I think we carried thirty-two kids in that workout. We identified the top sixteen boys and girls. Even if some of them swam JV in the swim meets, they all worked out together. We had ten lanes and split the kids, with me reserving the right to put the kids in the lanes I wanted them. If I had too much socializing, then I would separate swimmers. But mostly, I tried to put the kids in their lanes according to ability.

This was all happening when the country was focused on women's rights and women's equality. Coach admits there was some resistance on his part to the movement—and on the part of many male coaches.

We felt we were being encroached upon by Title IX—that no one knew what it was going to mean. It was like someone opened a door and jammed his or her foot in. Here's what happened: early on, many women—empowered by feminism—didn't understand what it took to produce a championship swim team. There were very few female swim coaches then. The job takes up a lot of hours—many early morning, weekend, and evening workouts. And believe me, there was no generous monetary reward for that commitment. Some swim club coaches made a little more than high school coaches, but you were never coaching to rake in dollars. You coached because you were motivated to coach, and you wanted to coach.

Early on at Foothill, two of the girls' physical education teachers signed on to coach the GAA (Girls Athletic Association) swim team. When Title IX happened, they demanded equal pool time to the boys' team. They wanted morning workouts at 6:00 a.m. and afternoon workouts until 5:30 p.m.

Wait a minute. Prior to Title IX, these coaches' whole experience had been GAA, which had never competed at the level and intensity of the boys' program. It had always been a more social activity—less focused on the swimming than the boys' swim team.

Eventually, Coach was called on to take over the girls' program; parents and others demanded the same intensity of training for the girls as the Foothill boys were receiving.

> All over the country, that was what happened. When the leagues started going coed, the boys' coach generally took over the girls' programs. There were some exceptions. There were some good female coaches, and I remember coaching against them. El Toro High School, for example, had a female coach. Now there are more good women coaches—and a few who coach both the boys' and girls' teams.
>
> When we integrated the boy and girl swimmers, we got absolutely no pushback. The hormones are going crazy. The guys were happy that the girls were there and vice versa. I had no problems in that regard. The parents were also very supportive. By 1976, we had established the program to the point that we had to turn swimmers away. Recruiting kids to come out for the team was never an issue.
>
> Our girls' teams certainly did as well as the boys during the 1970s. They won, I think, thirteen league championships in a row. We never won CIF girls' swimming because of Mission Viejo and the huge age-group swim program down there that feeds the high school. But we did win the CIF relays a few times. It was a real competitive program. From about 1978 through the early eighties was when the girls' program really took off. We ended up having some really fine swimmers. A lot of them were coming to us from the SoCal program. I think that between 1978 and 1993 when I retired, we had four dual meet losses and eighty-four wins. The boys went eight or nine seasons undefeated, and the girls had a run of seven undefeated seasons. And we swam everybody. We didn't duck away from any teams. That was a very fun time for me in terms of seeing the kids be successful.

Coach remembers many of his girl swimmers and divers very fondly.

> From sixteen seasons coaching the FHS girls' aquatic teams, I enjoy many great memories of working with some really wonderful young women. Laura Reynolds was a team leader and a high school All American. Other outstanding swimmers included: Julie Reynolds, Rhonda Reese, Deidre Mazurie, Lauren Birney, Adrian Schuessler, Megan Logan, Sionainn Marcoux, Laura Ellison—and so many, many more! I also coached some outstanding divers like Tina Coffee, Linda Koval, Kathy Cummins and Tina Summerl.
>
> To tell you the truth, having to make lists like this—for both my girl and boy athletes—makes me very uncomfortable. As I filter through my memories, I feel humble remembering all the many outstanding young people whose paths have crossed mine. As I think about them, I realize that a book telling those stories would be far more interesting than this book about me!

Seventeen

FOOTHILL FAMILIES

The sport of swimming is one where the whole family often becomes involved, and most, if not all, the children in the family compete. Foothill's swimming community had many such "swimming families"—and over the years, Coach became good friends with many of the parents. The Furniss family is one example.

> I became very good friends with the whole Furniss family. The dad, Bill, was, of course, so instrumental in the building of the Foothill pool. Chip was on the first Foothill boys' team, and Steve and Bruce were Olympians.
>
> I started picking up Chip Furniss—the family home was right on my way into Foothill—and giving him a ride to morning workout. When Steve came along—the brothers missed overlapping by a year—I starting picking him up every morning. They both loved to tell a story about my old yellow Porsche. When I'd come down Seventeenth Street, and I'd turned to go on the street where they lived, I'd goose my car a couple of times. They would hear that, and then they'd always be right out by the mailbox waiting for me.
>
> Later, I took Bruce to school every morning for workout. Then Craig overlapped with Bruce. When I picked up those two, Craig was the more studious one. I can remember all three of us in my car. Bruce would be in the middle, and Craig would have this huge book bag. This was before the backpack era. Can you imagine all three of us—and the books—crammed into my little Porsche? Bruce and Craig—to this day—love to tell stories about those rides.

Pat Furniss, the mom, was also special to Coach. He remembers being at the house when she died. He knew that she was failing, and so he'd gone over to the house after school that day. Later, he remembers that he was a pallbearer at her funeral. Coach's memories of Pat are all fond—and one of them makes him laugh to this day.

> Pat and I had been close since my very early days at Foothill. We had to do some crazy things in those days. We couldn't find any decent team suits in the school colors. So, we bought some white Speedos with the idea of dying them. I went over to Pat's house after practice one night,

and we dyed the Speedos in her washing machine. We dyed them gold. Actually, they turned out a putrid light yellow.

When the kids got in the pool with them, the suits looked transparent! They weren't transparent, but they looked like it when they were wet. When you would see someone swimming in the pool with one of these suits on, you would swear they had nothing on! Pat and I got the biggest kick out of that. We laughed for years about our naked Foothill swimmers.

Coach's own family qualified as a swimming family, with his mom, Peggy, becoming very involved with the team. After the "naked suit" incident, Peggy's sewing skills were called on.

I remember that my mom made our first water polo caps. In those days, the caps didn't have ear guards. They were very similar to the lifeguard beanies worn by lifeguards in Australia as well as to the caps worn by junior lifeguards at beaches around here. When I went to order the caps for our first water polo season, I discovered they were backordered for six weeks. So, I took an old water polo cap to my mom, and she got some duck material and made water polo caps for us—a set of black and a set of white. That was pretty cool. I mean, we had cheesy numbers sewn on—we looked pretty amateur—but they did the job, and it's a super, super memory!

The Furniss men have hosted a monthly lunch get-together for many years. Before their dad passed away, the brothers decided they wanted to get together regularly to take their dad out to lunch. Very soon after this started, they decided that it would be fun to invite a mystery guest.

Having had the opportunity to coach all four of them through their entire high school careers, I was the mystery guest on a few occasions. Before the guest arrives, the inviting brother will give hints about who the guest is. Sometimes, if I couldn't attend the lunch, they would call me from the restaurant. Whoever is on the phone would say, "OK, we're at lunch, and I'll give you three guesses who our mystery guest is." A lot of their mystery guests are former teammates from Foothill. It's just a lot of fun.

Even after their dad died, the brothers continued this once-a-month lunch. I have always admired them for making time for family like that. It's important to all of them, so they make time for it, even though they are all very busy and successful.

Another important family from the seventies was the Wills family. Chris and Kenny Wills were both very competitive swimmers for Foothill. These days, Coach takes pride that Chris is one of the doctors who has made him into the "bionic man" he is today—with two artificial knees and one artificial shoulder.

The parents are Bob and Maralys Wills. Bob is a retired attorney and writer. Maralys is an author who teaches at Orange Coast College. She's written numerous novels. One, *Higher Than Eagles*, is about hang gliding. *A Circus without Elephants* is another book she wrote about her family.

The Wills have also been a special family to us, and we have been close with them for a long time. Kenny Wills was just an exceptional swimmer who graduated Foothill in the early seventies.

Splish Splash

Tracy Wills swam for me on the swim club—the Foothills Fins—when I started that team. She was a great swimmer as a seven- and eight-year-old. Then she got really hooked on tennis and ended up a remarkable tennis player.

Coach remembers the dignity of the Wills family in the face of great tragedy. Two of their sons died while hang gliding.

One of the Wills boys, Eric, was a swimmer; the other son, Bobby, was not. All the Willses were great risk-takers, and hang gliding was something all the boys did. The death of those boys was a great shock and loss to everyone at Foothill.

The Reynolds family included seven kids, and six of them were Foothill swimmers.

I had a Reynolds in the pool for me—it seems like forever. Laura Reynolds was the oldest child, and she was the first of the Reynolds I had through the program. She was team captain and really an outstanding swimmer—a real leader—and I had so much fun with her. Ed Reynolds was second; he was an amazing swimmer. He may not have had as much natural talent as some swimmers I've coached, but he overcame his lack of talent with sheer effort. He became a really outstanding contributor to our program. Julie and John were twins, and they were also outstanding. Probably the best swimmer in the whole family was Mike. He was exceptional, an All American swimmer. Laura made high school All American; Mike was high school All American. Robert was the last Reynolds through the program; Kathy was the youngest and the family's only nonswimmer.

When Robert, the last Reynolds, finished swimming at Foothill, the family gave the De Longs and the Simcoxes (their Foothill coaches) an all-expenses-paid trip to Acapulco as a way of expressing their appreciation.

It was their way of saying thank-you to David and me for what we'd done for their families. David had all the boys through his water polo program, and of course, he was assisting me the whole way with swimming. We coached together for many, many years. It was a complete shock to all of us. And neither the Simcoxes nor Clara and I ever talked much about that trip to anyone. Right now is probably the first I have really acknowledged it in any public way. It was such a grand gesture; nobody wanted anybody thinking it was anything more than something nice the Reynolds family could afford to do for us.

A favorite memory for both couples in Acapulco occurred at a hotel fiesta they attended when they first arrived. There were lots of games to play. One was darts, and the dartboard was mounted on a column—not a wall. Clara was up to play. She threw the dart, and it missed the board—and the column.

Just as Clara was asking where the dart went, a guy walked around the column with the dart sticking in his cheek. He says, "Here's your dart, lady."

Well. We ended up seeing him again at the farewell party on the last day of our stay. Clara ran into him and said, "Oh, I hope you're OK."

He said, "I spent the last four days in the hospital." Turns out he was joking, but he didn't tell her at first, and of course, she felt just horrible. Finally, he grinned and admitted he was kidding. The dart didn't do a thing to him. When we get together with the Simcoxes and reminisce about old times, that story always comes up.

The Palchikoff family was also important to Coach. Jan, Kim, Kai, and Jay Palchikoff were all involved with Foothill aquatics. Coach knew the family from his years coaching at Sammy Lee Swim School with Lee Arth.

The Palchikoff family was one I knew long before I even walked on the deck for the first time as coach at Foothill. They swam for me at Sammy Lee's.

One time I remember is taking them home from a swim practice, and the house was locked. I lifted the sliding glass door out of the track so they could get in. They were all freezing—so it's a good thing I was such good friends with their parents!

Coach remembers all the Palchikoffs fondly. Kai was a stalwart on the beginning Foothill water polo teams. Jan went on to row for the United States in both the 1984 and the 1988 Olympics Games and has been inducted into the UCLA Athletics Hall of Fame. Jay Palchikoff and Coach remain great friends to this day.

The Hastings family was another one that Coach knew from his years at Sammy Lee's. One of the daughters, Laura, was a nationally ranked butterflyer during Coach's first years at Foothill, and he invited her to work out with his Foothill varsity boys.

When we did a kicking workout, Laura and Susie Whitaker just killed everybody else in the pool. I have always said that girls are better kickers than boys—partly because of their different ankle structure. Girls are more flexible.

Sharon Hastings is the oldest of the children. She swam for me at Sammy Lee Swim Club. She was a hard worker and a dedicated swimmer. In the summer, when I was running the Learn to Swim program at Foothill, I hired her as a swimming instructor. I remember I assigned her to teach my wife to swim. She had more success working with Clara than I did!

Coach had a close relationship with Mike and Mark Hastings, who were both divers. Eventually, they partnered with Coach in his clown-diving act. Both Mike and Mark remain close friends with Coach and his family.

The Hastings boys started diving with me all the way back to the time I was coaching at Sammy Lee's. Mark was just ten or eleven. Lee Arth wanted both the boys to be swimmers because they were good. But they both wanted to be divers.

We had a divers' relay team in all our dual meets. Diving was always held after the fifty free; they'd take the lane lines out and hold the diving competition. But I would always make my divers swim. Mark—who was a C at the time—was a really good butterflyer. In my mind's eye, I can still see him up on the starting block with his diving suit on, swimming the butterfly, which was right after the diving. The other divers would be on the deck, drying off and relaxing—feeling good about themselves—and here was Mark, swimming in the next race.

Both brothers, of course, had to swim on the divers' relay team; they had to earn their keep.

Mike and Mark spent a lot of time in diving workouts with me. I remember the day I introduced them to the ten-meter tower at Los Coyotes Country Club. You have to understand that once you're up on that tower, it is way more of a challenge than it even appears. The horizon line blocks the pool. In the mind's eye, there is no water below you.

I told the boys to just jump the first time up; both were nervous. Mike went first and made it just fine. Mark was younger and even more nervous. He was taking a long time. I shouted to him, "Mark, I'll count to three—and then you jump. One…"

Instantly, he yells to me, "You're counting too fast!" That memory makes me laugh to this day.

Dr. Myrt Hastings treated Coach's kids, Ty and Courtnee, for allergies. Coach remembers the medical office being down near Fashion Island in Newport Beach. Ty and Courtnee had weekly appointments.

A great story I have is about Billie Hastings. She would come to all our swim meets, and most times, she followed our swim bus. She drove this fancy black Corvette, and those were the days when the national speed limit had been lowered to fifty-five miles per hour. Well, here she is in her sports car limited to fifty-five. So, she made this sign that she could hold up for other drivers to see. It was two backward fives, so in someone's rearview mirror, it would read correctly. When someone was going too fast, she'd flash that sign at the driver. The kids on the bus would see her do it, and it just cracked them up. She had that fancy sports car, and that was just cool.

The Summerls were a swimming family with whom Coach had a long-standing relationship and great memories.

Tina was a diver—she was a very good diver. The oldest son, Dale, also dove and ended up getting third in CIF diving one of my first years at Foothill. Dan was a breaststroker and freestyle sprinter. I got to know Dick and Lois, the parents, quite well. They are a family who was certainly inspirational to me early on.

To this day, the Sadaro family remains an important part of Coach's life.

Dave Sadaro swam for me, and I grew very close attachments to his family. Dave's dad was an avid sailor, and his boat was one of my earliest rides. I sailed in quite a few races on it—some longer ones, including a couple to Ensenada. The boat was named the *Andiamo*, which is an Italian word whose meaning is similar to adios. Dave kept that boat for quite a while after his dad passed away.

Coach also speaks highly of the Drucker family.

Dana Drucker was the girl who designed the Foothill Aqua Knight logo. She had two brothers and a younger sister who swam. For the last few summers, I have had Leslie's three kids—Leslie was the younger Drucker sister—in my home pool learning to swim. That's been fun for me because I have reconnected with that family.

Clara De Long is the *cuma* to Steven Salata. Cuma means godmother in Serbian, and the Salatas are Serbian. Both Steven and Jason swam and played water polo at Foothill.

Jason was ASB president. Both went to the Naval Academy and played water polo there. Jason made his career in the navy and has been very successful. As the spokesman for the U.S. Navy Seals, Jason has drafted speeches for both President Obama and President Trump about the Seals. He presently serves as Spokesman and Director of the Office of Communication at U.S. Special Operations Command in Tampa, Florida. Steven served eight years in the U.S. Navy, worked in national intelligence jobs in Washington D.C., and is now a corporate vice president at Comcast, a Fortune 50 entertainment, media and technology company.

I had the chance to do a Tiger Cruise with Jason when he was stationed on the aircraft carrier CMN 68 on the USS *Nimitz*. The *Nimitz* was the flagship for the Pacific Fleet. I got to go on that cruise with my great friend and body-surfing legend Fred Simpson. We went from Bellingham, Washington, to San Diego, California. It was just amazing.

I also did a Tiger Cruise with Steven from Hawaii to San Diego on the USS *Boxer*, which is a helicopter and harrier amphibious attack ship. I was in line for breakfast on that ship—in the officers' quarters—the morning of September 11, 2001. We got a message that an airplane had crashed into the Twin Towers. Their ship's satellite communications were down just then, and we were getting intermittent communications. Everyone at first thought it was a private airplane. About a half hour later, we heard about the second plane, and immediately, the whole ship went to "Threat-Com," which is one of the highest alerts. Not really understanding what was going on, we were joking that the only way the terrorists could get to the ship was on a magic carpet!

Both cruises were absolutely incredible. The one on the *Nimitz* had us up on the observation deck watching takeoffs and landings. The pilots are required to do a certain amount of training each day. Flights are called sorties. During the time Fred and I were on the *Nimitz*, pilots were doing extensive training.

Every single takeoff and landing is filmed and evaluated. They have three restraining cables on an aircraft carrier. With the middle cable, the pilot gets three points; the first cable, he gets one point; and the third cable, he gets two points. There is an ongoing competition during deployments.

A perfect landing is on the second cable. The first cable is too close to the end of the deck, and there have been mishaps. The last cable also means a less-than-perfect landing. When the wheels touch, the pilot goes to full power. So, when the jet hits the restraining cables, it is at full power—just for a moment—until the pilot knows that he has hooked. If he misses the hook, which we saw happen, then the pilot simply takes off again. That's why they have to be at full power. If the pilot cut power, and he missed the restraining cable, then the jet doesn't have enough momentum to fly—and it goes into the water.

We had plugs in our ears—with big ear protectors atop them—and the roar was still unbelievable. The air right in front of you makes your skin shake. You're maybe sixty or seventy feet away from where all these jets are landing. You're not on the deck—you're elevated above on the superstructure of the aircraft carrier. That was just an incredible experience.

Eighteen

Water Polo

Because the Foothill pool did not open until 1967, the high school did not field its first water polo team until the fall of 1967. Coach had a talented bunch of swimmers, but most of them had never played water polo before.

> When we first started water polo in 1967, most of the kids played in the first game they ever saw. I remember I used to take as many of those kids as I could stuff in my car to Belmont Plaza to watch Cal State Long Beach water polo games. They needed to see what the game looked like. When I first started coaching water polo, I did what a lot of other coaches did. We got John Wooden's book *The Pyramid of Success*, and I modified the basketball drills so they'd work for water polo. There were many similarities between the two sports. Of course, water polo has changed dramatically over the years. It has probably undergone more rule changes than any other sport. Water polo today is vastly different from when we started our program at Foothill in 1967. For example, in the early years of the water polo team, probably ninety-five percent of my swimmers would turn out for water polo. Today, many athletes will choose one sport over the other.

Weight training came to the fore for swimming in about 1960 or 1961. Prior to that, coaches believed that weight training was the worst possible thing for swimmers because it would knot their muscles. They equated weight training with Mr. Universe—big, slow-moving muscles. Coach remembers that he first started weight training at the University of Denver in 1961 to 1962. When he came to Foothill, his kids were unable to do weight training the first year because they were training off campus at Three Cs Swim School while the Foothill pool was being built. Coach had that pool for only two hours—there was not enough time to both swim and lift weights.

The next fall at Foothill, when the water polo program was established, Coach began weight training for his athletes. Typically, they would train Monday, Wednesday, and Friday mornings and be in the pool on Tuesday and Thursday.

Coach, always the great competitor, remembers those early days.

Tom De Long with Sharon Hastings

Early on—before I got to be an old-timer—I was always the strongest person in the weight room. My swimmers tell me now about some of my exploits—when I was bench pressing three hundred and ten pounds—and putting to shame my strongest kids! I remember one time that I beat Bob Richards in arm wrestling. I had the respect of the whole football team because of that! But I have always been a gym rat.

A bit later, Coach got his swimmers training with surgical tubing. They would do swim pulls out on the deck—and other exercises with the tubing—for fifteen or twenty minutes before they got into the water.

We even swam against surgical tubing. A swimmer would have the tubing around his waist, push off the wall, and swim until the tubing held you in one place. We did that until we discovered that destroys your stroke! For a stroke to develop properly, a swimmer must be moving through the water. If you're static in water, then you're using different techniques than you do when you're moving the water. It gets complicated, and it was fun for me to fool around with the science of swimming.

Bernoulli is the inventor of the propeller. Bernoulli's principle shows that when you're swimming, your hand doesn't just enter the water and pull straight back—it makes an S pattern as it goes through the water. If you dissect a butterfly pull and a freestyle pull, they are almost identical. The difference between the two is that when you're doing butterfly, your body is flat in the water. But you're still doing an hourglass figure with your hands. Two things are happening. First, your hand is not moving straight back; it's moving somewhat sideways. You're actually cutting through the water similar to the blade of a propeller. Then there's a term called "new water." New water means that the molecules of water are static; they're not moving. Once you get them moving, the propulsion part of moving a swimmer through the water isn't as efficient. In a nutshell, that's the explanation for why a swimmer makes an S-pattern stroke. My job was to coach the science, knowing that I'd put kids to sleep in a heartbeat if I spent too much time explaining the physics of it. But this was all new stuff just coming out as I began my coaching career. I'd go to swim clinics and just be a sponge.

When Coach first began water polo at Foothill, there was great crossover between swimmers and water polo players.

Having been around water polo for many years prior to coaching it, it was a natural progression to have two sports and to run a water polo program. I always wanted water polo to be in the spring and swimming in the fall. It made more sense to get kids in really good shape swimming and then to play water polo rather than the reverse.

But because water polo is a fall sport, some schools saw some kids only play water polo. We started to have that problem but not too much. Particularly, as a kid becomes a senior after playing water polo in the fall, he may choose not to swim in the spring. If he's come up through age-group swimming, then he's been swimming for more than ten years. By that time, he has a lot of high school friends, and the spring of your senior years has an awful lot of fun activities associated with it. So, even at Foothill, we saw some drop out then.

Some of the swim coaches have to really, really fight to keep their kids in swimming—particularly in their senior years. If a kid is just a so-so swimmer—middle of the pack, you still desperately need those kids to win dual meets. They score five places, and those middle-of-the-pack swimmers can make all the difference.

When they scored only three places, you could do well with a real small team. But now they have A and B relay teams—and the B team earns points. The change in scoring did two things. It required that you have a little bit bigger team. And it also gave those middle-of-the-pack kids more reason to take part. They knew they were contributing to the team—even when placing fourth or fifth.

As soon as the scoring changed, swimming became, to my mind, more of a team effort rather than an individual effort. In my mind, this blended well with the team sport of water polo.

Nineteen

Olympians

Coach's first Olympic swimmer was Steve Furniss. He was an outstanding high school athlete for Foothill, and one of his accomplishments has never been replicated. Steve won two CIF championship events as a C, two as a B, and four swimming varsity. In his four years, he won eight individual gold medals in CIF, including a couple with relay teams that won gold. His specialties were individual medley, backstroke, and freestyle.

Steve graduated from Foothill in 1971, and we won CIF that year. He made the 1972 Olympics in Munich, Germany. That was the infamous Olympics where all the Israeli athletes were killed. Mark Spitz was the premier swimmer of those games. Steve has many stories of that horrible incident that happened in Munich. He was a bronze medal winner in the two-hundred-meter individual medley.

Steve's younger brother Bruce also accomplished something that has never been replicated. Bruce took Steve's world record away from him in the two-hundred-meter individual medley.

When Bruce broke the world record, the existing world record holder was his older brother. It's inevitable that records will be broken; so who better to do it than your own brother? It's nice to keep a world record in the family.

Both Steve and Bruce made the 1976 Olympic team. Along with the Furnisses that year, Foothill alum Rod Strachan was also on the team.

Bruce won the two-hundred-meter freestyle, beating John Nabor and setting a new world record. He swam a leg of the eight-hundred-meter freestyle relay to a gold medal and world record.

Do you know what's really amazing? Bruce has really bad spinal arthritis—to the point that, many times, he could hardly get up from a seated position. He suffered from his sophomore year in high school on. He did all the things that he did—ten world records, either relay or individual, and he was several times national champion in two different events—all the while suffering from spinal arthritis. Many experts say that the affliction definitely limited his achievement. What an accomplishment!

In 1976, Rod Strachan won the four-hundred-meter individual medley and set a world record.

Bruce won the two-hundred-meter freestyle. I always say that of the four Olympians I had the privilege to coach, we ended up with four gold medals and one bronze medal. A gold medal for Bernie Wrightson, two gold medals for Bruce Furniss, one gold medal for Rod Strachan, and a bronze medal for Steve Furniss.

Steve and Bruce Furniss and Rod Strachan were Olympic swimmers who swam in Coach's Foothill High School program in the 1970s. Their success influenced the public perception of what was going on at Foothill.

I don't think coaching them added pressure to the program, but it created a firestorm of interest. I've always said that success breeds success.

We had fifty-plus All Americans through our Foothill program—a whole host of outstanding athletes who've gone on to become outstanding adults—which is maybe the most satisfying part of the whole experience for me. When I hear from my former athletes and learn how successful they've become, that's one of the great pleasures of my life.

This is a joy of coaching in an aquatics program. It just seems that the kids who come through aquatics become very successful.

Twenty

The Results of Foothill Olympic Success

The Olympic Diving and Swimming Committee has a national high school representative. It's more of an honorary position, but the high school rep does get to vote. Coach served on the committee from 1972 to 1976. Sammy Lee and Pat McCormick were also on the committee.

> I remember I'd always vote the way that Sammy Lee or Pat would ask me to vote! The issues then were about how the next Olympic trials were going to be conducted: what are we going to use for qualification standards so you don't have four hundred divers diving in the prelims? Those standards changed even more dramatically after I was involved.

In swimming, certain time standards qualify swimmers for the Nationals or the Junior Nationals. They are sometimes called cuts—timed trial standards that a swimmer has to meet or exceed. In diving, the standards are decided by a point system. A diver has to demonstrate certain competencies. If a diver wins a national championship, then he or she is automatically qualified.

The committee also votes where the trials will be held. Different venues apply to host them—just like cities apply to host the Olympic Games. As a member of the Olympic Committee, Coach was involved in that selection.

> For the 1976 Olympics, we chose Cincinnati, Ohio, to be the diving venue. Many of the folks who served with me on that committee are deceased now. Of course, Dick Smith was involved as well as Jerry Darda. One man, who I won't name, had a daughter who was an outstanding diver. He was a multi-multimillionaire, and he wanted the Nationals to be held in his town. He built a complete facility there just to host them. He was influential on the committee because of his wealth. His town is where we had the Nationals but not the Olympic trials. Politics end up in all kinds of things, I guess.
>
> He was the principal funder of the facility—and really, he did it for his daughter. So, that's kind of cool.

Coach found it interesting and fun being on that committee. It was also an opportunity to travel.

Splish Splash

In the winter we had a meeting at West Yellowstone where we got to go on some day trips on snowmobiles into Yellowstone National Park when nobody was there. I remember we rode around by the hot springs where all the buffalo would gather. We had a convention in Washington D.C. My sweet Aunt May flew up from Florida. We spent two days doing The Smithsonian. That was a memorable time.

Twenty One

Teaching Stories

While at Foothill High School, Coach spent the school day teaching. During his more than thirty-three-year tenure, he became good friends with many of the Foothill teachers and tells fond, funny stories about them. He has particularly good memories about G. B. Ward.

> For a time, G. B. Ward's kids had an FM radio station. One of the great stories that we older Foothill teachers tell—when we get together and we start cranking out stories—was what happened when Ward got the license to have a low-frequency FM station. The students had a morning news broadcast on it, and then they played music. I think the signal strength was for a distance of about a mile. It was an introduction to broadcasting for the students.
>
> Somewhere, Ward got one of these crank-up towers like the ham radio operators have. He got permission to fasten it to the edge of the building right by the door to what was then the metal shop. He needed a pole cut into pieces in the form of two X's to run wire to make an antenna. Ward decided to see what he could find on campus.
>
> Ed Doyle, who was the band teacher—the "Music Man"—had a marching band that used a pole to mount a banner they would carry during parades. The flag girls would carry this banner at the front of the band announcing the Foothill High School Marching Band. As the story goes, one Saturday, the band was to perform at some parade—maybe Tustin Tiller Days. They arrived in the morning, and as they loaded their instruments into a big van, they couldn't find the pole for the banner. Somebody said they'd seen G. B. Ward with the pole. It was then they discovered it had become a part of the radio antenna!
>
> Soon after, Ed Doyle was at a faculty meeting. He stood up and claimed his turf. In no uncertain terms, he announced that nothing from his music department was ever to be touched again by outsiders. Even after all these years, we older Foothill teachers still get a lot of mileage out of that story.

Another G. B. Ward story that Coach loves to tell involves a starting pistol.

> In the mornings, we had a ten-minute snack break with a five-minute passing. If you were going to have a cup of coffee at the cafeteria, then you had to hustle. Well, G. B. Ward would come zipping down at break to the coaches' office to use the restroom. Then he'd go out the

side door that opened to the alley and cut right across to the faculty dining room—maybe fifty or sixty feet away. He was very predictable.

One time, we were in the coaches' office, and I gave Ward probably fifteen or twenty seconds in the bathroom before I opened the door into the locker room, took my starting pistol, and fired it! Of course, the room is mostly tiled, so the echo was very loud. He came storming out, just red faced, and blasted out the door.

Right by our door was the school intercom phone—everything in those days could be dialed with just two digits. I picked up the phone and dialed the faculty cafeteria. My timing was perfect. Just as Ward opened the cafeteria door, the phone—right there by the door—rang. He picked up the phone and barked, "Ward, cafeteria!" Into my end of the line, I said, "Bang!"

That's another story that made the rounds for quite a while. All the coaches really had a lot of fun with that.

Coach remembers and admires Mr. Ward for an innovative teaching aid he devised.

He took a Union 76 gas station ball—somehow he got ahold of one—and he made a true work of art. He took the ball apart. Even then, half the globe was too wide to go through the classroom door, so he had to adjust the ball so that the cutout part at the top and bottom would angle against the door jam. He then rotated the thing into the classroom. It was pretty ingenious. He got it into the classroom and put it back together.

He had the metal shop teacher build a frame that was tilted at twenty-three and a half degrees—the tilt of the axis of the earth. He put a handle on it, so you could spin the whole globe around. This was perfect for showing earth/sun relationships. Right in front of the class, you could spin it to show the first day of summer—with the North Pole tilted twenty-three and a half degrees toward the sun. Then you could show where the direct rays of the sun would fall at the Tropic of Cancer. You could then turn it to show where the direct rays would fall on the equinox at the equator. Spin it farther, and you'd expose the Southern Hemisphere where the Tropic of Capricorn is located.

He had a geography class, and with his strong direction, they put in all the continents and oceans and the grid of longitude and latitude—showing the three hundred sixty degrees of the earth. He used it to demonstrate time zones. It was so creative, and it was such a great teaching tool—probably one of the best teaching tools ever used at Foothill. It was all just right there. So, if you wanted to talk about plate tectonics and earthquakes and all the things we covered in geography—well, here was this absolutely terrific physical model.

This story just goes to show you how creative G. B. Ward really was. We had a lot of fun poking at him, but we all respected his creativity.

Another Foothill teacher about whom Tom has great memories was Taylor Wagner, a history teacher who also coached C football.

Taylor was another "character-character." He came from Tennessee. He always had all this homespun philosophy going on out on the football field. I remember him out there yelling to his kids, "Bow that neck! Get stiff like a wagon tongue!"

Wagner, Coach recalls, had been a marine aviator and had been on an aircraft carrier destroyed by the Japanese in World War II.

> He spent nineteen hours in the water. Sharks were eating his colleagues several feet away from him. But he survived the ordeal. He told me he took all his clothes off except for a ring that he had said would never come off his hand.

When Mr. Wagner was teaching history and covering World War II, he took extreme pride in coming to class in his flight suit.

Wagner, Coach remembers, had contracted tuberculosis and had part of a lung removed. But he remained an avid runner. High school students sometimes underestimated him.

> He'd yell, "Get off that lawn. Come here, young man." The kid'd take off running, and Taylor would take off after him and just run him down!

The coaches at Foothill were a close-knit group—especially in the early years. Most were in their twenties or early thirties, and they liked to have fun.

> My first two or three years at Foothill, we had a Schoolmasters party. It was held at the Osterman Ranch way out in El Toro—out in the orange groves. They had a room there that would probably seat sixty or seventy people. I remember it was rustically furnished and had windows that would open out—it was almost like being in a stable or a small barn. The coaches would go out there, drink beer, and play cards once a year. It was Foothill and Tustin—just the two high schools—and we called it Schoolmasters. Good memories come to me from those early years. I keep returning to this theme—it was an innocent time.

In those early years, the men and women coaches at Foothill were both adversaries and friends.

> This was before Title IX, but we still interfaced with the women coaches in physical education. We didn't do coed—they had their program, and we had ours. It seemed like there was always fighting going on. The women were very possessive of their stuff—as we were of our stuff. Yet we all got along really well. We had several social functions a year. There was a traditional after-the-football-game party at one of the coach's houses every week. We rotated that around. That was something that everyone went to—and there didn't seem to be intersport jealousies among the coaches. We had a lot of fun. I still have close relationships with many of the coaches who coached at Foothill during my tenure there. We have a breakfast four times a year where we see each other and catch up. Everybody looks forward to that—and now, of course, what we best like to do is brag about the grandkids!

Twenty Two

Coaching Colleagues

Coach was privileged to work during a golden time of competitive swimming, and he coached alongside some remarkable age-group and high school swim coaches. In particular, he has immense respect for Lee Arth.

> Lee Arth—I was in awe of him. When I became coach at Foothill, he'd won the previous four consecutive CIF championships at Fullerton High School. He had Andy Strenk and the Webbs. He had some incredible swimmers.
>
> Lee was soft-spoken—easygoing—a very good technician. I never wanted to be a yeller and a screamer. My yelling and screaming was enthusiasm; it wasn't putting kids down or being harsh to them.

Coach had the chance to coach with Lee Arth when the Orange Peels were split off from the Anaheim Sammy Lee Swim Team. Lee was the head coach; John Urbanchek was also coaching there. The Orange Peels worked out at the Three Cs Swim Club on Tustin Avenue.

> Lee Arth had a different coaching philosophy than many of the coaches then coaching. He asked for more quality, rather than quantity, from his swimmers. He'd have them go shorter distances—asking for better-quality performances. He had really good results.
>
> Swimming workouts used to be about getting in the pool and grind, grind, grinding away. They really weren't that effective. I think all us coaches took things that we were learning at clinics and other places in the world and changed the way we coached. That was the time that cyclical training started. Hard effort, short rest; hard effort, short rest. That type of training began to replace the idea of getting in the pool and just swimming for yardage. Lee was an early adopter of cyclical training. He also gave me a lot of good information about swimming. I was a diver; I wasn't a swimmer. So, I became a student of the sport, and he was very helpful to me.

Coach admired both Lee Arth's coaching results and coaching style. It resonated with an idea Coach knew about from the Marine Corps—the difference between demanding respect and commanding respect.

> I'd tell my students and swimmers that in the Marine Corps, your drill instructor would demand that you respect him. If you don't, then he will kill you! I told my kids, "I want to command your respect. And to command your respect, I first have to earn it. Earning your respect is something that I'll work hard to do." That's the core philosophy that I had—something I learned, I have to say, by observing coaches like Lee, whom I admired, and from observing successful teachers.
>
> I've spent years and years teaching swimming to little kids, and I know that you achieve your best success when "you kill them with kindness." Once a little kid trusts you, everything else is just a piece of cake. And to get to those who have a harder time getting on board, I say, "We never lock the gate to the swimming pool; you don't have to be here. You need to be here because you want to be."

Another very important colleague for Coach has been his fellow Foothill coach David Simcox.

> I first met David when he was a young guy at Santa Ana College. He'd been in the navy, and he wanted a job teaching/coaching. While David was at Santa Ana College, their pool broke down. The coach, Bob Gaughran, who'd been a national-level water polo player, went around to various schools to ask whether his team could workout with their high school teams while the college pool was repaired.
>
> I knew Bob because, during the summer, he ran the swimming program at Red Hill Tennis Club. So, I took two of his swimmers; David Simcox was one of them. They swam with us for maybe a week or ten days. Nice guys—but naturally, I was most concerned with my swimmers. As I remember, David understood and told me, "We'll just do your workout; don't mind us."

David left Santa Ana College, served in the US Navy, and then went to Cal State Fullerton, where he finished up his degree. He began his student teaching at Santa Ana Valley High.

> One day, David walks in and says, "I've really got a problem." Well, I did remember David—but it had been a couple of years. He refreshed my memory about swimming in my workouts.
>
> Santa Ana Valley is a pretty rough school. David had been there for just one day when he drove to Foothill and asked me, "Oh man, can you get me here? I'm at Santa Ana Valley, and I know I'm going to get in a fight." So, I went right up and saw our principal, and David became my first student teacher.

By the time David began his student teaching, the aquatics program at Foothill had grown enormously. Coach had been solo for a long while, and he needed help.

> I'd been coaching alone all this time. I had Hank Hummel help me one year, but that was not a permanent situation. I really needed some help. So, I went up to talk with the principal, and of course, there was no teaching position available. But I kept going in and kept hounding him.

That summer, a job in special education opened at Foothill.

Splish Splash

David had zero background and zero courses. So, I got him a glossary of terms and told him to cram. The plan was for him to go in and interview for this job. Dwight McCracken, who was the principal at the time, was helping us out on this, hoping that June Felder, a Foothill teacher—ex-military, a drill sergeant, tough as a nail—would interview and hire David. On the day of the interview, David was all set. He'd been studying this glossary of terms. As he's sitting there waiting for the interview, he saw his two competitors who were both special ed experts with extensive training and credentials. He looked at them and said to himself, "What am I doing here?" He was feeling like a fool.

As David was waiting for his interview, he got a call from Dwight McCracken, the principal. Bill Snyder, a Foothill football coach, had abruptly resigned and had taken a job in Texas at a community college. [Bill Snyder is currently head football coach at Kansas State University, and the school's football stadium was recently named after him.]

So, Dwight McCracken decided to fill that coaching void with David Simcox. It was a full PE assignment—not one bit of special education. He had that full PE assignment for only a couple of years, and then they put him into a classroom. But he was so happy to be where he was and to get the job that he got.

At the time David joined the Foothill program, Coach was head water polo coach. The first year, David acted as assistant coach.

But I was nervous that he'd start looking elsewhere because he wanted to be a head coach. So, the second year, I said, "David, you do the water polo; I'll do the swimming. I'll be your assistant in water polo and you be my assistant in swimming." So, we were co-coaches and that's how the program worked for several years.

I remember once that the school district wanted either David or me to take the head coaching job at Tustin High when they put the new pool in. The superintendent called me in and said it would be really important for me to take the job down there. One of my quotes always was, "If you cut me, I bleed black and gold." So, I said no, and David had no desire to go to Tustin. He'd been head water polo coach for a while, and we had a really good thing going at Foothill.

Eventually, Jim Brumm—who also did his student teaching at Foothill—joined the aquatics program at the school. Both David and Jim assisted Coach with swimming, and all three coached water polo. Then, David gave Jim the water polo job. After one season away at Santa Ana College, David came back and coached at Foothill after Coach retired. Since 1965, there have been only three coaches in the swim program at Foothill High School. When Coach retired in 1993, David Simcox succeeded him as Foothill swim coach. In time, Jim Brumm succeeded David.

I was very fortunate to work with a great team of coaches my entire career. I didn't come up with this quote, but it's out there: "If you're really, really happy with what you're doing, then you never have to work a day in your life." I've always believed that. I've never had a job, I believe. If you say that to people, and they don't know you, they'll look at you funny and say, "What?"

I just look back at them and say, "I played for thirty-three years."

The years Coach was at work may have been optimally fun ones for him. Diving has since diminished in importance as a high school sport.

> They don't dive in the high school meets anymore. Foothill High School's brand-new pool is only eight feet deep with no diving facility. That tells you what's happened with diving. A lot of it is about liability. They still have diving as a CIF event, but it's conducted on a separate day, and then they just take the diving points and apply them to the team totals. Sometimes at meets, they'll do a diving exhibition where the top six divers will dive during a quick break in the meet. But diving is no longer part of high school swimming programs in the way it used to be.
>
> It's sad, really. I can understand the insurance issues—everything in the world has become more litigious these days. And not having diving in swim meets speeds up the meets. Still, diving is a beautiful sport performed by skilled athletes. It's too bad it doesn't have the showcase it used to have.

Foothill High School's First Swim Team, 1966

Splish Splash

Coaching Water Polo

Coach at workout, 1981

The 1974 FHS team, winners of four straight CIF championship trophies

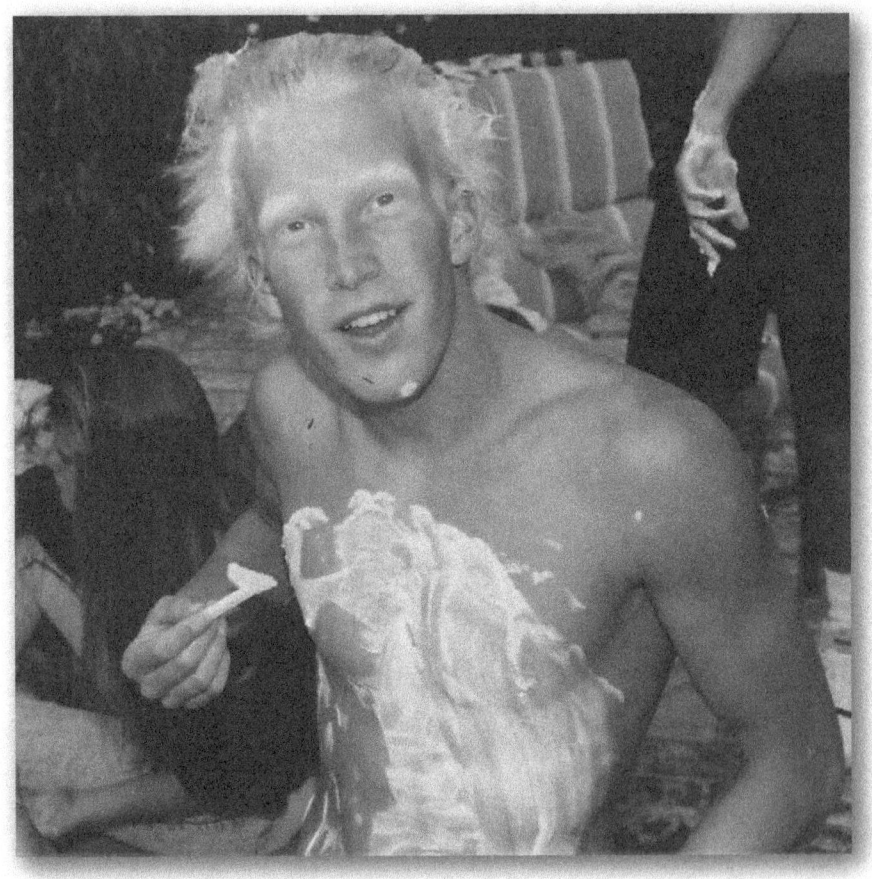

Marc Hansen at "Shave Down" party

Splish Splash

Bob Bonebrake scoring with an early morning prank

Coach called them "The Four Freshmen"—Four FHS swimmers who made Varsity as Freshmen

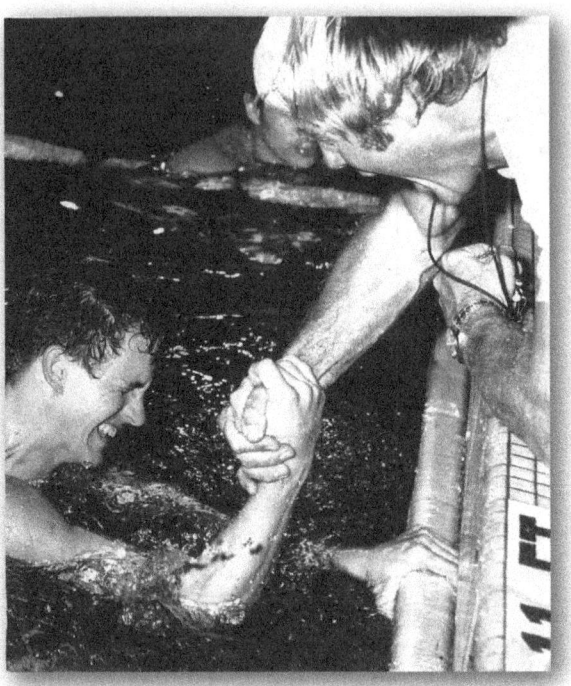

Bruce Furniss sets national high school record in the 200 yard Individual Medley

Coaches De Long, Jim Brumm and David Simcox winning 1989 CIF Championships

Splish Splash

Coaches De Long and Rick Rose

Mike Hastings begins a inward dive

Jason and Steve Salata

The Furniss Family: (L-R) Chip, Steve, Bill (Dad), Bruce, Craig, Pat (Mom)

Twenty Three

The Tom De Long Family

On July 4, 1965, Coach and Clara moved into their first house. It's the home where they still live. Their first child, Ty De Long, was born on August 4, 1965, just before school started. He was born in Palm Hospital in Garden Grove.

> Ty was born in the afternoon. He had a ton of bright-red hair. When I first saw him, the nurses had combed his hair and put a part in it. And he had a tooth. At that time, when a child was born with a tooth, it was called a milk tooth. But here's the funny part of the story. When Courtnee was born, she was born short a tooth! Now, tell me that's not a good story!
>
> Ty was the talk of the hospital. Here's a baby born with a mass of bright-red hair and a tooth. When Clara first saw him, her comment was, "This isn't my baby. You've made a mistake." They assured her that there had been no mistake; Ty was ours. One of Clara's friends brought her a baby toothbrush.

Coach was lifeguarding that summer awaiting the start of his new job at Foothill. Clara was teaching in the Newport Mesa District, and—even with the birth of their new son—Coach proudly recalls that she didn't miss a day of school. She taught all the way to June. Ty was born in August, and Clara went back to school in September.

> We had a great gal who took care of Ty: Amanda Jones. She lived two-hundred feet from our house. She'd come over in the morning, and Ty didn't even have to be up. She did laundry and light housekeeping for us. She was a middle aged lady; I think her daughter was a junior in high school. Ty ended up being in the daughter's wedding as a ring bearer when he was four. That family was real special to us. In fact, I ended up teaching both of Amanda's granddaughters how to swim. She passed away a few years ago, but she was very dear to both Ty and Courtnee.

Coach remembers it was a very busy day when their daughter, Courtnee, was born at Hoag Hospital.

I'd started the Foothill Fins, and I had a swim meet the day she was born. She was born early in the morning, so I was there for the birth and then was able to get to the swimming meet. To this day, Clara says that had she not delivered when she did, I'd have probably missed the birth of our daughter!

Ty started school at the De Long's neighborhood school. But when he entered first grade, Clara transferred him to the school where she was teaching. Having Ty near Clara greatly helped the working couple balance the dynamics of careers and child-rearing. Eventually, Courtnee also went to that school.

This was a more innocent time when you could let your kids walk places. Emil Neimi was a famous coach and referee in Orange County. His wife did after-school childcare, so the kids would walk to their home after school. Clara would pick them up after she got off work and take them to whatever activities they had—or they'd come home.

Coach has great memories of the years when Ty and Courtnee were young.

We thought that we had died and gone to heaven with the camping we did. We bought a Coleman tent trailer, and we had a 1969 Oldsmobile Vista Cruiser station wagon with the windows all around the top. There was a gal whose husband was an officer in the military. He was sent to Vietnam, and he felt so bad for his wife that he went out and bought her the most expensive station wagon on the market. It ended up that they had to let it go; I guess financially they couldn't handle it. And they almost gave it away. So, we got that car, and we thought that it was the coolest thing. It was blue with wood-grain panels. I had a trailer hitch put on it, and I hauled our tent trailer with it.

For nineteen years, the De Longs traveled every summer to Colorado to visit Clara's mom. They would always make a vacation of it and stay en route at a national park. They had a particularly memorable time at Yellowstone, after which they wandered back roads down to Colorado.

Those were the days before mandatory seat belts. I'd make the whole back of the station wagon flat, and the kids would have their own sides. The fights that'd ensue because somebody encroached on somebody else's space were memorable just on their own.

Coach delights in some of the crazy adventures his family had traveling and in some of his crazy inventions for his kids.

I guess that the inclination to take risks may be part of my DNA. Our one rule is that when we camped, we had to camp where there was a really tall tree. When we got our lane lines for the pool, we had no use for the crib line that we had. It was a cool rope, so I snagged it and took it home. I used it to make my kids a swing. I'd climb as high as I could in these tall trees, get the rope over a branch, bring it down, tie it off, and usually put an aluminum folding beach chair on it. I'd fashion a harness so that the beach chair could be at the bottom of the swing.

Splish Splash

I'd get the kids in there, tie them in, and gave them the swing of their lives. The higher you arc the swing, the bigger the swing is. I can remember I had swings that were fifty feet above the ground. That was one of our important camping traditions: we'd have to camp where there were trees tall enough to accommodate our rope swing.

Another unique toy developed by Coach for his kids came from an idea he got from Bob Wills. The family called it the high bike.

Bob had built this bike, and when he came by the pool at Foothill, he was fully above the block wall. The seat, I think, was eleven feet off the ground. He'd welded two or three bike frames together and two or three different chains to reach up to the crank.

So, I took a bicycle frame and turned it upside down so that the crank was nearly up as high as the seat. Then I got some copper tubing, put the seat up high, and extended the handlebars. My kids would launch themselves from the fence by our driveway and ride around on that thing. You'd either have to stop them, or they'd have to pull onto the grass to slow down and let the whole thing fall over.

Another toy developed by Coach was a hit with his kids and the whole neighborhood.

One year for Christmas, I got this idea. I built them what I called the egg. On a four by eight sheet of plywood, I drew out the largest egg shape I could make. Then I put the two pieces together with crosspieces and had a carpeted seat in there with a seat belt. It had handles to hang on to. I rimmed the whole thing with hose that I split so that I would have rubber tracks to roll on. As the egg rolled, you'd go upside down, and you'd be turning summersaults. But it was devised in such a way that you could pump it like pumping a swing. So, you could keep yourself going. That egg was the hit of the neighborhood for a very long time. The kids would take turns—and away they'd go down the street.

The reason I made all those things was so that the kids would have a lot of fun—risk-taking really wasn't on my mind. We didn't spend a lot of money, but we sure had fun. At one time, Ty wanted to be a stuntman. When he was a sophomore in high school, his full intention was to be a stuntman in the movies.

The kids in Ty's school would have field trips to Supai, which is located in the western part of the Grand Canyon on the Havasupai Indian Reservation. You go thirty or forty miles past Kingman, Arizona. Then it's about a six-hour hike to get down into the canyon.

We've tons of pictures of the kids jumping down there. They launched off super high cliffs into a beautiful pool of water that is very deep. Both of my kids would jump from the highest point that you can jump into the pool. For several years when she was in high school, Courtnee jumped from the highest point of any of the girls. She was a great gymnast—I always knew that both my kids had inherited the "risk gene."

Twenty Four

Extended Family

Christmas was always a very special time for both Coach and Clara as they grew up. When the kids were little, the De Longs traveled to Colorado two or three times to spend Christmas with Clara's folks. Coach remembers that Clara's dad died in 1967, and the family spent the Christmas of 1966 with him and Clara's mother.

> Clara's dad was one of those guys who'd go to the back of a magazine and order all his medications. He never went to the doctor. But his gall bladder went south on him, and he went in for gall bladder removal. He said, "I'm really worried I'm not going to come out of here." Even at that time—1967—gall bladder surgery was not a major concern. But he developed a bleeding ulcer and died as a result of it. He was seventy-two.
>
> Clara's dad lived through the Depression, and he led kind of a tough life. He was in World War I. I think he died too young. I know that my mom at sixty-three died too young. I have some memories of that time that are bittersweet.

The family continued to go back in the summers to visit Clara's mom. She would also come out to California to visit. When she began to develop a bit of dementia, the De Longs moved her into an eldercare facility near them. She had problems with blood circulation and had to be on a blood thinner.

> I think she probably developed pneumonia because of that. She was eighty-three when she died. She'd had numerous surgeries, so her overall health was not good. That's why I think that pneumonia was what led to her death. Had she been stronger, it might not have been as serious for her as it was. This was 1982 or 1983. Both Clara's parents were older when they had her. Her mom was forty-three or forty-four when Clara was born. Back in those days—1938— that was very old for a woman to have a child.

The De Longs' warm and welcoming home is decorated with many family heirlooms. They have a foot pedal sewing machine that belonged to Clara's grandmother. Clara doesn't sew on it, but the machine is operational. Another prized heirloom is an old Firestone Air Chief radio—an upright

Splish Splash

console—that also came from Clara's family. Clara has great stories about listening to *Boston Blackie, The Inner Sanctum, Amos and Andy,* and *Fibber McGee and Molly*—all radio shows from when she and Coach were young. This was, of course, long before television.

Coach hopes that the family heirlooms he and Clara have enjoyed will pass on down through the De Long family. He, himself, has added to the trove of family treasures.

For each of the ladies in my life—my wife, my daughter, and my daughter-in-law—I've created curved-top, cedar-lined trunks. When we redid our family room, we had old California cedar shelving. I took that, milled it, and built Clara her trunk. Later, I made one for Courtnee and for Kindy, Ty's wife. I entered the one I made for Kindy in the Orange County Fair and won a ribbon for it. That trunk—because I entered it in the fair—required a big envelope taped to it with my picture, pictures of me constructing the trunk, and a little bit about the trunk. That was fun. But I have to say, those trunks were very intentional. I've built them to be heirlooms.

I've also built for both my granddaughters three-story dollhouses. They're shingled, the walls are pickled, there are hardwood floors, and the windows are very detailed. All the roof shingles are hand cut. There's copper flashing for the rain gutters. I spent hours doing these—a real labor of love. I made one for Anika, and then I made one for Abigail. The dollhouses are on custom-made lazy Susan tables. On Anika's, there's a little flower pot on the front porch that has a dowel below it that locks the dollhouse down. If you want to spin the dollhouse, then you lift up the flower pot, and the house will spin on its lazy Susan. There're six rooms, and there's easy access to the front and back of the house.

Twenty Five

The Next Generation

Ty and Kindy De Long

Ty De Long served as ASB president at Costa Mesa High School. The summer before his senior year in high school—as the incoming ASB president—Ty attended the Southern California Youth Citizens Seminar at Pepperdine University. Student leaders from all over Southern California were invited to attend. Ty won an award for a group presentation and was asked to speak at the closing ceremonies.

> After his high school week at Pepperdine, Ty just fell in love with the school and came back and said to me, "Dad, I really want to go to Pepperdine."
>
> It's *so* expensive. But we decided we'd see what could be done. Dr. Charles Runnels, the director of the Youth Citizenship Program, was chancellor at Pepperdine. Ty made an appointment to talk with him, and I went along. Dr. Runnels was very impressed with Ty. Ty told him that he really wanted to go to Pepperdine and wondered if there was any scholarship funding available. Halfway through the interview, Dr. Runnels looked over at me, and he said, "I think we can come up with half…" Well, what can you say? It was still going to be a big bite, but I said, "That sounds great. That's doable."
>
> Over the next four years, Ty worked several jobs on campus and eventually became a resident assistant, which took care of his room and board. He then got another scholarship—and then another. I believe that when all was said and done, Ty got almost ninety percent of his schooling funded. He took out a small student loan that was paid off a few years after he graduated. We were so impressed with and proud of him.

Ty De Long met Kindy Pfremmer when they were undergraduates at Pepperdine. They were both English majors and had several classes together. Throughout their undergraduate careers, they were good friends, but neither was interested in pursuing a dating relationship.

After graduation, Kindy took a position recruiting accountants, and Ty completed a teaching credential and began teaching at Agoura High School. After a year there, he was offered a teaching position at Colegio Maya, an American school in Guatemala. Because of some administrative issues, Ty eventually canceled his contract there and applied to Pepperdine to pursue graduate work in English. He was offered a full scholarship to do so. During his last month in Guatemala, he received a letter from Kindy letting him know she would also be at Pepperdine in the fall to pursue a graduate degree in religion. Within a year, Ty and Kindy were dating.

> They just decided to be a couple. And you know what? They're still the best of friends. That's what's really neat about their relationship. They have so much in common and get along so well. As parents, Clara and I feel super blessed.

In May 1992, Ty and Kindy were married. As they completed their graduate studies, they balanced school and work. Ty took a job at a middle school in the Oak Park School District. He taught full time for several years: English, history, and technology classes. Eventually, he took a position at the district office as director of technology. Kindy worked at Pepperdine, teaching classes in western civilization and religion. She then took a two-year position as a visiting instructor in religion.

Both Ty and Kindy enjoyed their work but gave it up when Kindy was awarded a presidential scholarship to earn her PhD at Notre Dame. The entire family took the opportunity to move to South Bend, Indiana. Evan was seven years old and Anika was four when the family moved east.

Ty and Kindy had decided to homeschool their children. Kindy began the process in California, but when they moved to South Bend, Ty took the lead. He took several odd jobs while the family lived in Indiana, but his primary work was teaching the kids.

When Kindy finished her degree, she was offered a position at Pepperdine as a New Testament professor. Ty had maintained good contact with his former employer during the five years he was in South Bend and was offered a part-time position when the family returned to Southern California. Ty's intent was to divide his attention between his teaching work in Oak Park and the continued home education of Evan and Anika. During his third year back at the district, Ty began working at a relatively new school in the district, Oak Park Independent School (OPIS).

Oak Park is an innovative district that had recently made contacts with independent study students. Some were working in movies or television. Others were elite athletes who live in Oak Park or neighboring school districts. Several of these students elected to earn an accredited high school degree through OPIS while pursuing their acting or athletic careers. Ty works each year with nearly thirty of these students, designing and administering their entire curriculum.

> His OPIS kids are really amazing. He has one woman who was a dancer in New York City. She and Ty were in contact every week, and Ty gave her all her assignments. Two former students in the schooll were Olympic gymnasts Gabby Douglas and McKayla Maroney. He has ice-skaters and actors—kids whose schedules don't allow them to have a traditional high school experience. The OPIS program has been very successful, and now there are eight full-time teachers involved. Ty is enjoying his work very much. He's been able to combine his love of technology—with the great experience he had homeschooling Evan and Anika—and has put together a program that's now helping many other kids.

Courtnee and Kevin Hein

Courtnee De Long and her husband, Kevin Hein, fell for each other on the dance floor. Kevin was in the Marine Corps at Camp Pendleton. Courtnee and a couple of her friends were really into line dancing. There was a place up near Disneyland called Cowboy Boogie, a nightclub. The girls started going up there to line dance.

Kevin and some of his buddies ended up there one night, and he and Courtnee met. I guess they met again three of four times there. Then he asked her out—and the rest is history.

Those two have a fine relationship. Courtnee and Kevin live in the Midwest—very different from Southern California—and she and her family are thriving. Clara and I love to visit them and are so proud of all they have accomplished.

Kevin started working at a factory after his time in the Marine Corps. Now he has been working for the last sixteen years in the gas and oil industry. He has moved up the ladder from an operator to a shift foreman to a training coordinator. Presently, he is the process safety manager for Marathon Petroleum Corporation.

Because of his work at Marathon, my son-in-law, Kevin, is more of what's known as a gentleman farmer. He has seventy acres of corn and hay. He also raises Jersey cows and chickens. In the summer and fall, he has a huge pumpkin patch and garden. Kevin just loves to be outdoors riding his tractor.

Courtnee is a skilled hairstylist. Coach says proudly that she retains five or six clients from her time working at an exclusive Newport Beach salon before she moved to Ohio.

She styles those women whenever she visits home, and she's just amazing. She has great talent. Had she stayed here, I think the sky was the limit. But, thank goodness, she didn't because she's made such a great life for herself with Kevin and her family in Ohio.

Courtnee has been working in town for twenty-three years. She's in a place called the Market Street Salon. Market Street is the main street in town—an old-fashioned street paved in brick. The salon is in an old building that used to be the town's hardware store. It has the old hardwood floors; it's really charming.

Courtnee—like her aunt, grandmother, and dad before her—is a talented craftsperson. She has made a cottage business in Minerva, Ohio, of her crafts, which include many crocheted and fabric items. There is great demand for them. She has a personalized tag on each hat or scarf. Her business is called Hein Homestead Farms. The tag has a little barn with a silo on it.

Courtnee, I think, would love to have her own craft store. But she works as a hairstylist in Minerva, and she has a very loyal clientele. She works three days a week, and this allows her to control her schedule. If she wants to come visit us in California, then she can have one of the other folks in her shop cover for her; but mostly, her clients just wait until she gets back.

It is pretty amazing how my mom and sister are kind of channeled in Courtnee. Mom was an accomplished seamstress; and of course, my sister was a very fine hairstylist.

Coach and Clara believe they are fortunate to have become good friends with the other sets of parents in the families both Ty and Courtnee chose.

> We've been blessed by both of the families our kids have married into. Dale and Cloyes Pfremmer, Kindy's parents, and Frank and Connie Hein, Kevin's parents, are wonderful people. Clara and I are really fortunate to have good relationships with all of them. There have been so many times when Dale and Cloyes have been at Evan and Anika's performances. And there have been equally as many times when Connie and Frank are sitting with us at Courtnee's kids' events. It really makes it special that we all like one another so well. I think when the grandkids look back, they'll realize that many grandkids don't have that.

Twenty Six

Grandchildren

The De Longs value their family and have always tried to be supportive parents and grandparents. They prize their close relationships with their children and grandchildren.

> I never want to put myself in the position of telling my children how to raise their kids. We just feel so fortunate that our children are doing the jobs they are doing.

Coach feels that he and Clara have learned important lessons from their children. As public school teachers themselves, the De Longs admit to being uncertain when Ty and Kindy decided to homeschool their children.

> We were concerned they weren't going to get the socializing they would in public school. But the family belonged to a home school association, which added a lot to the homeschooling experience. I know many people have an attitude toward homeschooling that says that the parents aren't qualified as teachers. All the parents are really doing is giving their kids books and telling them to read them. You'd be completely impressed to see how these parents teach—to plan out the week and then to follow through. It is just amazing. Both of my grandchildren are extremely bright, and they're doing very well. Through their home school association, they did field trips. Our granddaughter was on a gymnastics team. Evan was involved with his church group and in the orchestra. So, they had plenty of opportunity for socialization. Clara and I have really changed our attitude about homeschooling.

Confirmed Californians that they are, Clara and Tom feel they've also learned from Courtnee and her family.

> Our daughter's children, growing up in Ohio, are getting life lessons far different from what they might get if they were growing up in Costa Mesa, California. They have lots of animals, and they live closer to the land than those of us out here. Then there are the benefits of living in a small town—where kids are known, and everyone looks out for them.

Splish Splash

Ty and Kindy De Long's Children Coach says that Ty's son, Evan, has been a violinist almost his whole life. Evan was six years old the first Christmas that Ty and Kindy spent in South Bend. Ty had taken Evan to a string quartet concert at one of the libraries in South Bend.

> All of a sudden, Evan decided he wanted a violin for Christmas. Kindy's parents bought him his first violin, which is called a one-fourth or quarter-size violin. We have video of when he opened the violin. In the video, Evan is just dancing, jumping up and down. "I know what it is. I know what it is! It's a violin!" When he first put it up, he put it up backward. He put the neck against his throat. It was very cute and very funny.

Ty and Kindy put Evan in Suzuki School. It's the practice at the school to put all the violin students in a line where they are taught the fundamentals of the instrument.

> That was also super cute to see. I remember Evan's first musical event. He played "Twinkle, Twinkle, Little Star"—a classic! There are Suzuki books—I think seven—and the kids progress through them, building their skills. They learn to read music. Evan, I think, made it through six of those books before Ty and Kindy placed him with a private instructor.

By the time Kindy finished her doctoral program at Notre Dame, Evan had been playing the violin for five years. He had been a part of the youth orchestra and had played with a string quartet. He had worked with a private instructor for nearly three years. When the family returned to California, they were able to secure Evan a wonderful violin teacher, Mrs. Joyce Osborne.

> She was fabulous. With her, Evan was able to progress on and on. He had the opportunity to play with the adult orchestra. There was a program for which the kids auditioned, and then they were picked to play solo parts with the Thousand Oaks Philharmonic out of Thousand Oaks. He's also had his own recitals.

After graduating from high school, Evan enrolled at Indiana University, where he studies at the Jacobs School of Music.

> He's done extremely well there. Clara and I recently went back to see his junior recital—the students do junior and senior recitals—and I don't think I am being just a proud grandpa—it was off the charts!

Anika De Long has also enjoyed considerable success with her music. She is an accomplished gymnast as well.

> Anika excelled at gymnastics—maybe taking after her aunt Courtnee—and she competed at a high competitive level for four or five years. But it got to a point where she was involved in just too many things. Like her brother, she's very involved in music. She also has pursued the violin and has done quite well. She's been involved with the Los Robles Children's Choir in

Thousand Oaks. She also sang with the state and national honor choirs. Now she's a voice major at Pepperdine University. Clara and I have enjoyed her performances very much. She's had a couple of solo parts where we've both actually gotten goose bumps.

Coach reports that Clara and Anika have a very close relationship. They FaceTime two or three times a month.

Anika will set her phone up somewhere in her room and then visit with Nana as she cleans her room or has lunch or something. It's very special, I think, for any grandparent, when a grandchild chooses to hang out with them.

Courtnee and Kevin Hein's Children Owen Hein, Courtnee's eldest, has been an athlete from day one, reports Coach.

The small town the Heins live in—Minerva, Ohio—is all football all the time! Owen began playing football at a young age, but then he discovered soccer. Owen's not a huge young man—maybe not big enough to have played football at the level he wanted. But the kid's really, really fast. He developed unbelievable skills as a soccer player. He played all the way through high school. After high school, Owen went on to community college. He's a really vibrant young man. He's flourished in the small-town environment; there are so many cool opportunities there that aren't available in big communities.

Eli Hein followed in Owen's early footsteps and has pursued football, playing for the high school team. Eli is clear that he wants to be a farmer—and a diesel mechanic.

The kids are all involved with 4-H. Eli's just a real farmer at heart. His dad has three tractors—and Eli can't wait for it to snow. The family has a long driveway, and Eli gets to ride a tractor and to plow the driveway. The newest family tractor has an enclosed cab with a stereo—very tricked out. Eli couldn't wait to tell us that he got to plow the driveway using the new tractor. Eli's just in heaven out in the barn or riding on a tractor.

The Hein's farm is very picturesque. There's a little stream that runs down behind the barn. Eli found out how to pan for gold. He has a sluice box; he also has a fort he's built down there. He spends a lot of time down by their stream. Even when it's freezing out, you'll often find Eli out there panning for gold!

Those kids have all had such great opportunities. They have had cattle and chickens and goats. There were about twenty chickens. I actually helped Courtnee build them a chicken coop so bad critters wouldn't get them. We made it out of an old tool shed. That was fun—especially since chickens were such an important part of my own boyhood.

Courtnee sent away for the chickens. UPS delivered them in a box full of holes—they were just little, tiny chicks. She raised them up, and they laid eggs like crazy. They're smaller chickens than the ones my family raised in Arkansas, and they laid brown eggs. Well, as it eventually always happens, the chickens stopped laying eggs, so the family got rid of them. Recently, they got new baby chicks. Both Eli and Abi are really involved with that.

Splish Splash

Abi Hein is the youngest De Long grandchild. She is a talented athlete and has inherited her mother's artistic gifts. Both Coach and Clara are enchanted by her.

> Abi is just her mom's little dream. Courtnee's very creative. She makes knitted and crocheted scarves and hats like you can't believe. She made lion hats—the high school is the Minerva Lions. Courtnee made these hats that look like a lion's head when they're on. The hats have ears, the whole works. Abi is always Courtnee's model. She looks so adorable when she wears all the things her mom has made.
>
> Abi's become an extremely talented soccer player. She, too, pursued gymnastics for about four years. Minerva has a great gymnastics program in the area—a few miles from their house. But then, she ended up following Owen—who coached her soccer team for a while. Abi has advanced skills in soccer; I can see her going a long way in that sport. She's just ten—our little one. She's been such a blessing in all our lives. Abi, like Courtnee, is amazingly talented as an artist. Her folks have her taking private art lessons. She's just quite a girl. Clara and I have been blessed in all our grandchildren.

Coach and Clara are fond and supportive grandparents. They often travel to see Courtnee's family. They value and enjoy family. It is fun for Coach to reflect on the similarities and differences between his grandchildren's and his and Clara's childhoods.

> In many ways, I see a lot of similarities between Clara and my childhoods and the ones these kids are having. That's particularly true of Eli. But you know, the electronics—video games, cell phones—do make it vastly different from when we were growing up. Those kids are so good with the video games; they do car racing—and they just blow Grandpa away. I can't begin to compete with them.

Twenty Seven

Woodworking

Coach developed his interest in woodworking from an early age. He had a couple of unusual experiences as a youth that contributed to his current expertise.

I never was a rocket scientist in school, so the easy A I could get in school was when I took a shop class. Every elective I had, I took a shop class. When I was in the eighth grade, there was a guy across the street from us in Long Beach who was a general contractor. He hired me in the summer, and he taught me everything—from bricklaying to setting tile to cutting glass. I was game for everything.

When my sister got my grandmother's house, she and her husband didn't want to use the garage for cars; they wanted to turn it into a party room. So, they just gave it over to me to remodel. I was in high school at the time—sixteen or seventeen years old.

By my standards now, my work was pretty crude. I built a bar for them. Rubber interlocking floor tile had just come out; I tiled the whole floor in that. Garages in those days had all the studs showing. I paneled the whole inside of the garage and the ceiling. It was done in plywood, which I stained and then varnished. It turned out pretty well and was a great party room for them.

When Clara and Coach were first married, he built some things for their first apartments. When they moved to their home in Costa Mesa, he continued his building and tinkering.

I've done this house two or three different times now. I've laid over five thousand bricks. I placed every brick on our property. I've dug fence posts. When we had the pool put in, I did all the tile—in fact, I've done the tile in the pool three times. I've tiled the spa and built a fountain. I bricked our whole deck. I've done all the tile in our kitchen and the tile in the bathrooms.

I do get accused of having an energy level higher than most. I enjoy doing the work. If I don't get to do woodworking for six weeks, then I almost go into withdrawal. I say to myself, "I've got to build something. I have to make something." I hope that desire doesn't go away anytime soon.

Splish Splash

Recently, Coach has been constructing lifeguard chairs.

> I had to do one for my godson's wife for a school fund-raiser—a silent auction. And I also did one for a silent auction for the centennial of the Long Beach Junior Lifeguard Headquarters. We had the centennial party on the *Queen Mary*. That chair went for over six hundred dollars. That was kind of fun. I made one for my friend who passed away, Raymond Bray, who started the junior guard program at Huntington Beach. It's at the Huntington Beach Junior Lifeguard Headquarters. There's a memorial for him there, and the chair is a part of it—with all his memorabilia from his years as a lifeguard and junior guard instructor.

Coach credits many of his skills to trial and error. Still, he is a careful craftsman.

> I'm a firm believer in cut once, measure four times! But I still have ten fingers. Some of them have been nicked and ripped up—I've been in the saw a few times. My doctor, Chris Wills, is the guy I call. And he always says, "What did you do now?"

Coach has "made the news" many times for his athletic and coaching achievements. But he has gotten ink for his woodworking achievements as well.

> I designed an addition for our home—a family room. I built a bed there that pulls out of the wall—it goes into an attic space. The facing of the bed looks like cabinets. Originally, I had the bed covered with rough-cut cedar shelving. I've since built a shelf with four fake doors. They even have hinges on them. You pull and out comes a queen-size bed—it comes out on rollers.
>
> When we have company, the family room becomes the guest room. We call it sleeping in the drawer. We'll have company over, and I have fun with them. I say, "Look around the room. Can you find a queen-size bed?" When they can't, I pull it out.
>
> My next-door neighbor was a writer for *Sunset* magazine. In 1989, the magazine was doing an article on guest beds, so they featured my bed in *Sunset* magazine. There's a three-picture spread of it in that issue. I remember the day the people from the magazine came to the house to do the feature. Gosh. They had all the umbrella reflectors. They had lights set up. They must have taken one hundred photos. That was really fun. I got a big kick out of that.

Twenty Eight

SAILING

Coach De Long's interest in and love of sailing is more than fifty years old.

Sailing—I have to be honest—was such a total and complete diversion from almost anything else I was doing in life. It became a time to switch off. It was very relaxing for me. Sometimes you have to force yourself to relax if you have a competitive nature. You can park your boat upwind and reverse your rudders, which causes you to just drift. The boat doesn't go anywhere; it's actually being slowly blown downwind. Then you just sheet in, go upwind, and park again.

But make no mistake—sailing is a competitive sport. Coach relished that aspect of it as well.

I can just remember being so cold. The afternoon wind would be blowing, and you'd be so cold even in a wet suit. Then boom! The horn sounds, the ten-minute flag goes up, and we're starting in ten minutes. Then another flag goes up at five minutes—going down at four minutes. You're sitting there shaking and freezing, and then—all of a sudden—the adrenaline is flowing, and you're having to get into position to get into a good start—and everything else goes away—you don't even think about it.

Coach recalls he started sailing in 1952. He would crew when he could. He got his first boat in 1979, which was when he started Hobie Cat sailing. He says he'd talked Clara into buying a boat and had ordered a twenty-five-foot sailboat from Shock Sailing. It could be trailered. It had a crank-up keel. It was a beautiful boat. He ordered it from the factory. But then…

We were down at Newport and out with some friends on a boat. This Hobie eighteen came cruising by us, and I said, "Boy, does that look like fun." I sailed a Hobie Cat in Mexico. Peter Spurzum's family had a place in Mexico, and they had a Hobie fourteen that I had sailed a few times. I had a lot of fun with it. So, I thought to myself, "I think I'll get a Hobie eighteen."

I was able to cancel my order from Shock Sailing; I think it cost thirty-five dollars. That was for the paperwork. So, I canceled the order on the monohull sailboat and bought a Hobie eighteen.

Splish Splash

> I started sailing it and then joined the fleet that was out of Long Beach and began racing. Then I got a brand-new eighteen. One of my swimmers at school, Brett Bainbridge, was from Australia. I learned that he had done a lot of catamaran sailing as well as Hobie Cats in Australia. I was looking for a crew, and he was little and strong. He started crewing for me, and he did so for almost three years. We couldn't do all the events because of our swim schedule. But we sailed together in the summers, and it was really fun.

Coach's first race was in Oceanside. He ended up being disqualified because he sailed through the start/finish line.

> The first time I raced, I didn't know too much about the rules. So, that was a real initiation. In Hobie Cat racing, you're going very, very fast. There are a lot of boats. It looks like there are boats everywhere—strung out. But you go two different directions—either port or starboard—but you can't go directly up to the wind. You have to go off the wind either way, but all the boats converge at a turning mark. You find out very quickly if the way you went was the best way to go!

Early on, Coach has great memories of the San Diego Classic. The race was held in Coronado, below the Coronado Bridge, right by the navy base. The afternoon winds blew down there just beautifully, Coach recalls.

> Back in the eighties, every event would have as many as thirty or forty boats in a class on the starting line. You can imagine there were a lot of crashes, a few injuries—I've been stitched up a few times. I almost had my Achilles tendon severed in one crash. I could see it—it wasn't cut—but I was filleted right open on the back of my heel. A standing wire from a Hobie sixteen did it when that boat T-boned my boat. There were a lot of collisions.
>
> If you got punched—the boats are fiberglass, and they're not real, real strong—little dings you'd work on yourself. For the more serious crashes, there are glass shops. I've probably spent several thousand dollars over the years in repairs. I once ripped my friend's boat apart and ended up paying for that. Oddly enough, you can buy insurance for sailing. If you have a complete loss of a hull, that can cost a couple of thousand dollars; there's insurance to cover that. And I've had that—I've had a couple of claims where I was able to replace an entire hull. You'd think they'd charge you a fortune if they knew you were racing—but I don't think the insurance companies really understand the violence of catamaran racing versus monohull racing. I think in the mind of an insurance agent—"Oh, a sailboat. It's only going five miles an hour."—but we're sometimes going twenty-five miles an hour.

Coach has made lifelong friends from sailing. Roger Jenkins—Coach ended up being the godfather to his son—was one of his early sailing buddies. Ted Lindley is another name Coach remembers fondly, along with John Hauser, Steve Leo, and Wayne Shafer.

Wayne has been an elder statesman of the sport because he was a close personal friend of Hobie Alter when they first started everything in Dana Point.

Beyond the ocean, Coach did a lot of lake sailing. He sailed at Lake Mead and Lake Cachuma. The farthest north he ever sailed was at Lake Tahoe.

> I've a lot of really fond memories; it's hard to pick one out. We used to use the term "racy." If you were racy, then that was really good. You didn't even care if you won or not—it's just the fact that you were competitive.
>
> There were so many exciting races, but the most exciting—I think—was down in Mexico one time. Ensenada is in the bay of Todo Santos. Down on the south end of that, we had an event every year called Todo Santos. I won a race down there, and that is one of my fondest memories. I beat a lot of really good sailors.

Coach has had a series of kids crew for him over the years. He has always had great concern for their safety.

> I'd caution for safety rather than risk-taking—something that might hurt the crew, someone else, or even me. I crewed with the kids for the experience and the camaraderie. If we got a bad start—or if we went the wrong way—then you could go a little slower and relax a little bit. It's pretty to look ahead and to see all those nice-looking boats.
>
> When you're in front, you're in trouble; every move you make, the boats behind you cover. And if you're not doing as well as they are, then they're closing the gap. Sometimes it's more difficult to be in first place than in fifth place. I learned a lot early on by just watching the boat in front of me—seeing if I could close on them. If I could close on them, then I knew I was doing better than they were doing.
>
> But I think this is typical of any sailor on any sailboat. I don't care if you're sailing a bathtub—if you sail up next to someone sailing a bathtub, then you have a race going! Somebody'll say, "Pull that jib in just a little bit, and we'll see if we can get this boat going just a little faster." I think it's commonplace with anybody sailing a sailboat.

A long race Coach remembers is what he calls the spring marathon. It featured a Le Mans start where someone would physically hold the boat in the water. Sailors would start down on the beach. There was a line. Each person would have to run up the beach, around a flag, and then back down to his or her boat.

> You take off, and now you're going forty miles. We'd sail from Long Beach up around a turning mark near where Marineland of the Pacific used to be. Then we'd come all the way back down to Seal Beach around a mark. Then we'd go out around three oil rigs that are twelve miles out called the Delta Rigs. You'd have to round all three of those. There was a referee boat—a power boat—to make sure that nobody cut. Then you'd sail back to Long Beach—a forty-mile round trip.
>
> It'd take two and a half to three hours, depending on how windy it was. If it was a windy day, then you could average—upwind, downwind, and across the wind—fifteen knots—fifteen to eighteen miles an hour. You're flying.

Splish Splash

What's really cool in that race is that going out to the Delta Rigs, we'd always pick up a couple of dolphins. They'd get right between your hull. There's a little thing that supports the mast and keeps the crossbar from collapsing, that's called the dolphin striker. It's on all catamarans.

Coach has many fond memories of sailing with dolphins.

The dolphins will get in the bow wake of a ship or sailboat. They love sailboats because there are no engines—and I think they know about propellers. They'll get in the bow wake of monohulls going to Mexico or Hawaii. Often, there'll be two or three dolphins. One night, I was on the sheet of the big spinnaker. I was down on the bottom, on the lowest side. The rail of the boat was about a foot from the water, and I was right down there. I looked over, and right beside me—literally, if I held onto the lifeline, I could have reached out and touched him—there was a dolphin. He was just looking me right in the eye—just sailing along. It was magic—just the best. There's nothing more fun than picking up a dolphin when you're sailing and then having it play with you for as much as half an hour.

Twenty Nine

The Transpac

Chuck Bittick was a very close friend of Coach's. Chuck met Frank Easterbrook, a very successful businessman who had a custom-made, seventy-eight-foot Lad, the *Ariadne*—worth over two million dollars. Ariadne is the Greek goddess who was sprinkled into the heavens and then became the Aurora Borealis.

Easterbrook had spent a quarter of a million dollars getting the *Ariadne* ready for the Transpac to Hawaii. She was a cruiser-class sailboat with a crew of twelve. The boat was in need of a crew, and Chuck Bittick introduced Coach to the owner.

The *Ariadne* is in a cruiser class called the Aloha class. Five guys sailed the boat around the clock. You're on five hours; you're off five hours; you're on four hours; you're off four hours; on three, off three—that takes you all the way around the clock. The owner was the navigator; his brother-in-law, who was a flatlander—a nonsailor—was the cook.

Coach sailed three long races on that boat to Puerto Vallarta, Cabo San Lucas, and on the 2007 Transpac to Hawaii.

The Transpac is on every sailor's bucket list. I was always fascinated by the idea of sailing it. It's run every other year. It's always run on the odd year. Many sailors have done it numerous times; it's a very expensive endeavor.

Coach tells great stories about the Transpac. At sixty-nine, he was the oldest person on the crew; the youngest crew member was twenty-two. Coach earned his place on the team in a race to Cabo San Lucas. He recalls that he was ecstatic when he saw his name on the list for the *Ariadne*'s Transpac crew.

Frank Easterbrook is an amazing boat owner. He's unbelievably concerned about the safety of his crews. We had to go to Safety at Sea School. Frank spent two hundred fifty thousand dollars just on the race on which I crewed. It was a thirteen-day race, but he put us through incredible preparation getting ready for it. We did a race to Cabo San Lucas, Puerto Vallarta, and

Splish Splash

Ensenada and many training sessions around Catalina. The training for the race took several months, and it was quite intense. We sought out extremely windy days so we could test our skills and test the equipment on the boat. Frank made sure we were well prepared for whatever we might encounter during the race.

Easterbrook did whatever it took to make the race a safe experience for everyone. Coach was impressed that he installed lifeboats on the *Ariadne*'s deck in such a manner that if something catastrophic happened, then the lifeboats would automatically eject and fill.

So, if we got broadsided by another boat—or hit a whale—then everything Frank could imagine had been done to keep his crew safe.

We were out there in the middle of nowhere for thirteen days. There was nothing besides horizon—three hundred sixty-five degrees of it. We did get into some storms, and you do that on purpose. When you get out into the trade winds, you see rain squalls coming at you. It may be blowing fourteen knots, but when the squall gets close to you, the wind velocity can go up to thirty or thirty-five knots. Our boat would be plowing along, but then we'd be able to hit twenty knots.

Frank had every electronic device known to man on the *Ariadne*; one allowed us to calculate where we were to a fraction of a nautical mile. We kept a log and measured the distance off the GPS. There was a competition between the two sailing teams about how far we went on each particular shift. We'd really work to log more miles when our team was on. Those were some of the things we did to keep the race interesting.

In a race like that, you learn some things. For example, if you want really good luck, then you have to kiss a flying fish on the lips. We'd catch them when they flew up and landed on the deck. We had a lot of fun.

Frank praised us by saying our team maximized the *Ariadne*'s potential—we pushed her for all she could handle. We got second in our class in the Hawaii race. We were the fifth boat to finish out of eighty-five boats. The owner was really pleased. He made us all a book of the sail, and on the inside cover it reads, "Wow. What an experience. Most of the race was beautiful. 20.5 knots and a second place finish were really a tribute to the capability and quality of the entire sailing team. Thank you all for participating with me in a lifetime adventure."

Clara and seven of the other wives flew to Hawaii to meet the *Ariadne*. In their enthusiasm, they illegally drove up a road to the top of Diamond Head, where they displayed a big finish-line banner they had made.

You come through the Molokai Channel. The wind really whistles through there, so it's very exciting. We finished at night. I was disappointed to finish then, but you finish when you finish. In the daytime, you're flying your spinnaker. The boats are just hauling. They come out with a helicopter, and they take photos of the finishing boats under full sail. Everyone on the boat is excited because you're almost finished. Everyone's on deck and doing their thing. So, in the daytime, they take these great pictures that are good enough to frame and display on a wall. But we finished at night, so we didn't get a finish picture. We didn't get to see the wives' banner either. They made it out of Hawaiian cloth, and it read "Ariadne." We took it to the banquet with us.

Each boat that finishes has a party for it. The marina, Rain Shop, sponsored the ending party for the *Ariadne*.

We finished at twelve thirty at night. By the time we got into the harbor and secured the boat, we were partying at one thirty. They have pictures of us coming in—we all put our team shirts on—and all the wives were there. A couple of guys came over who were friends of the owner. Thirteen days, eleven hours, thirteen minutes, and eleven seconds—there was a lot to celebrate.

Last photo of Coach's birth family, 1977
Rufus, Peggy, Coach, Marjorie, Paul

Coach with two tiny swimmers—from his 61 years of teaching swimming

Coach and lifelong friend, Fred Simpson, at Coach's induction into
the Hall of Champions at Long Beach City College

Coach displaying his craftsmanship in a 1989 article in Sunset Magazine

The De Longs: Clara, Tom, Courtnee, Ty

Coach and Clara with their grandchildren
(L-R) Owen, Anika, Eli, Evan, Abi

A training day aboard the *Ariadne*

Thirty

Philosophy

As you have read, Coach De Long has had a rich, full life. Through his many adventures and experiences, he's developed a set of principles and beliefs he's found useful.

Consistency

My grandmother handled her fair share of the disciplining. She wasn't a tyrant but she was extremely consistent. We toed the line—my cousins and I. There was a consequence there, and we knew it was going to happen! There was no negotiation.

Consistency was one practice both Clara and I valued throughout our teaching careers. I always admired Clara because she was always incredibly consistent with her students. As a result, she's got books and books and books of how much her kids loved her. Teaching was her passion—and still is.

When I was competing, you feared your coaches in those days—but you also had a tremendous amount of respect for them. You'd never challenge them—that was just beyond consideration. Whether you thought they were fair or unfair, it was a nonissue. That was the way it was.

Early on in my coaching career, I tried to be that way. But soon, I gained an appreciation for the words "command" and "demand." I'd often use those words at the beginning of a season or the beginning of classes I'd teach. "I'm going to attempt to command your respect rather than demand it. If I demand your respect, then you may give it to me, but you're not giving it to me with an open heart." My aim was to be fair—but also very consistent.

Risk-Taking

There are really two types of risk-taking to my thinking. There's physical risk-taking and there's risk-taking that's academic or mental risk-taking. Because I was a male who grew up at a certain time in the country's history, I was given a certain amount of free rein—it's something that doesn't occur today because we are living in a different time. I can remember being quite young and the only restriction we had was to be home when the streetlights came on. That freedom shapes one's personality, I think. I was always taking risks because I was so much on my own.

Coaching risk-taking is something that you do with divers and with kids who are just learning to swim. Teaching kids to overcome their fears is just something that you do step by step by step. Some coaches were more forceful about that than I was. I tend to go at a little slower pace—the same thing with diving. That's a really hard thing to answer. I think you just develop a philosophy—the way that you approach overcoming fear. I know that in sailing when you have someone crewing in a hairy situation where it's really windy and pretty scary, the approach to use is to try and build confidence gradually rather than just thrusting it on somebody all at once. I'm not a person who would throw someone in a pool and tell him or her to swim. It's the worst possible thing you could ever do.

Discipline

As times changed, kids had far less time at their disposal, and I saw that as I was coaching. But at Foothill, one thing I was very aware of was that there seems to be almost a direct correlation between self discipline and individual sports [like swimming, tennis, etc.] where you cater to a more motivated individual. I am not shooting down team sports, but football, basketball, and baseball have different kinds of kids playing.

In swimming, we catered to a kid who was more academically motivated than some of the other sports. I have said this numerous times, especially at clinics where I am asked to speak.

In swimming, we have kids who really learn how to budget their time. And to make sacrifices. They have to make choices that you as the coach hope they make in favor of their sport. They sometimes have to sacrifice going to a special concert because of homework and swimming.

As my career went on and on, I was able to tell my new swimmers about kids who'd been through my program who were extremely successful—who became doctors and lawyers and other sorts of successful careers. So, I could tell my new kids: "Here's what they did, and here's how they became successful." You never get to know what kind of an influence that kind of talk will make on an individual. But I'd tell them: "You have X number of hours in the day, so you have to make choices. If you're pursuing high-track academics, if you're taking accelerated courses, if you're planning to go to college, if you want to know how to write properly, then it takes time." I never told my kids that swimming was first; I always said to them that school had to be first.

I had kids I'd excuse from practice because they were getting ready for an SAT test or going to a pre-SAT class, and some of those classes were only offered at certain times. We made allowances in that regard. I always felt that was most important. And those kids always seemed like they would give me back more than I was giving them. I think my tendency to prioritize academics over sports was uncommon—even in those days. I know that I had not only kids but also parents who appreciated my philosophy. Even today, I still think that philosophy holds. If you follow kids who are really successful in swimming, then my bet is that there's a high percentage of those kids who excel academically all the way through college and beyond.

Competition

It may be that I seek out activities that totally involve my mind. I have never been an anxious person, but sometimes I can't sleep when my mind gets racing. I can remember getting sick the night before a big swim meet my first couple of years coaching. We'd go to a movie to try and burn some time—but still, I'd have to go out and find a Dumpster. I was never nervous as a competitor. I don't know what it was as a coach. But it was awful. That lasted only two or three years.

Through all that, though, I never lost the edge of enjoying the competition. I just loved what's called doping out a swimming meet. You know what the other team has, and you try and use your swimmers to the best possible advantage. The top times were always posted, as were meet results. I paid attention to them. In fact, during swim season, I subscribed to three different newspapers so I could keep track. I was recently going through a trunk of things, and I found articles from thirty years ago. Why the heck do I have this? It was meet results of Corona del Mar swimming against Garden Grove in 1969. I'd clipped the article then to save the swimming times so that I'd have them when we came up against those teams. That practice wasn't just me. All coaches did that—track, swimming, cross country—where there are results that are involved. You want to know how far someone is putting the shot or how high somebody is jumping. Kids and parents always like to see results in the newspapers—and the papers know that—so the results are there, and coaches take advantage of them.

But all that said, a lot of coaches—after they had retired—came back to me and said, "Boy, it was so hard to figure out what you guys were going to do. You'd always throw us a curve." Once you turn in your entries at the beginning of the meet, there are no changes. We probably won a lot of meets that we might have lost had we not swum the lineup that we submitted. If you know for sure what the other team is going to do, then you have an advantage. So, it was fun for me to always keep them guessing! We were always blessed to have enough versatility to be able to put swimmers where the other team was not expecting them to be.

In fact, I'd say that strategizing was one of the things I missed most when I retired from coaching. It was something I'd done—and had fun with—for the previous thirty years. I was successful because of strategizing—or maybe because I had more talented swimmers. I've always said that swimmers are made, not born, but equally, I know that coaching is sometimes highly, highly overrated! I really mean that. Too many coaches try and take too much credit. And they don't swim a stroke or throw the football or baseball. They try to take too much of the credit for the hard work the athlete does. I was always totally satisfied just feeling I was part of an individual's career.

Coming through the ranks when I did, everyone coaching—I don't care what the sport was—was influenced by two of the greatest coaches on the planet. One was Vince Lombardi, and the other was John Wooden. Lombardi, of course, coached football, and Wooden was at UCLA coaching basketball. John Wooden has an incredible philosophy while being fiercely, fiercely competitive. But he was a realist. Lombardi was probably the other way. One of his most famous sayings is used by everyone all the time, but he coined it: winning isn't everything; it's the only thing. In my opinion, that's very detrimental to the average athlete. An elite athlete can have that philosophy. An elite athlete hates to lose. But you can't win all the time. And I think it's unhealthy to have the attitude that, if I don't win, then I have failed.

We ran the full gamut of ability at Foothill. One year, we were proud to say that we had the fastest swimmer in the league and the slowest swimmer in the league. And everything in between. The more you can skew that number toward faster swimmers, the more successful you're going to be.

All kids can measure their success on a stopwatch—good swimmers and not-as-good swimmers. And every single one of them can improve. They can end the season swimming the fastest they have swum in their lives. And whether that is a time fast enough to score—it doesn't matter. They're heading in the right direction; they're improving. That's part of the selling point you have as a swim coach. A swimmer has an absolute way of measuring how well he or she is doing. You don't have that in some other sports. A swimmer who "owns" a time has something to challenge himself or herself with all the time. It's always there.

With a team, you'll have some extraordinary athletes, and then you have ones in the middle and ones who trail. For many years, my evaluation of a really good high school swimmer was somebody who could break fifty seconds in the one hundred freestyle and somebody who could break twenty-four seconds in the fifty. Now you'd have to say twenty-two seconds. And then somebody who could break one minute fifty seconds in the two hundred. I am talking about boys. Those are the times I considered really, really good-quality high school swimmers who are going to score—even today—in almost any dual meet. They'll contribute in your league championships. But for years, we'd have a celebration anytime a kid would break a minute in the one hundred free. So, a kid comes out for swimming, and he can swim—obviously, he can swim. He might even have a fairly decent stroke. But you work with him, and success breeds success. Everybody else seems to be going fast—so what the hell—I might as well go fast! Kids just start improving.

I was blessed to have many superstar athletes at Foothill. But I tell you, I made a conscientious effort my whole coaching career to make sure that the nonsuperstar swimmers felt a part of what we were doing. It paid huge dividends in all sorts of ways. It was a labor of love. I spent a lot of time doing things that perhaps other coaches didn't. For example, I painted the whole swimming pool. I hand painted the record board and kept it up to date.

Favoritism

Favoritism is something that happens from time to time. But I think the kids earn favoritism. Coaches and teachers are human, and they're naturally drawn to the kids who are working hard and giving their best effort. Kids who are loyal. Maybe you don't call it favoritism. It's just a bonding that happens between a coach and an athlete. I think it's an earned situation both ways. If a swimmer bonds to a coach, then I think, in some ways, the coach has often earned that bonding. And vice versa. It's almost a matching of intensity. As a coach, you really gravitate to the kids who're putting in the effort—who're doing what it takes to excel. It's the same way in a classroom.

Evolution of Coach's Thinking

Swimming parents can be wonderful—or not. I jokingly used to say, "The best coaching job in the world would be at an orphanage!" I know that I am not standing alone when I say this. Virtually anyone who's coached at any level, for any length of time, would say exactly the same thing. When you coach, you'll experience the whole spectrum of parents.

I had a problem with a parent one time. There was a kid who wanted to swim with the swim club. I had two Olympians—soon-to-be Olympians—plus a couple of CIF champions in the program. There were some unbelievable swimmers on the team at that time. Our workouts were incredibly challenging. So, this kid came along, and he started doing really, really well. He was club swimming in the off-season. What he wanted was to swim with his club—and then just come and swim in our swimming meets. I didn't allow that—I never allowed that in the whole time I coached.

This kid quit the swim teams after about three dual meets. His time in the fifty—he was a sprinter—was then the fastest in CIF. We went all the way through the CIF prelims and all the way through the finals, and the CIF champion won the CIF championship in a slower time than this kid had swum in our third dual meet. And he dropped off the team—and we still won CIF by forty points.

Another kid chose to transfer schools in order to work out with his swim club and not with the Foothill team. The principal backed me up completely. I told him, "This is the way I feel about it, and if you don't feel the same way, then you need to get a new swimming coach." And he backed me up. It was ugly with the parents and with the whole situation. This kid transferred schools. The next year, he came back to Foothill and wanted to be back on the team. I said, "No, I don't think so. You should probably just swim with the swim club." So, he did.

I do have some regrets. I know that the kid was ultimately the loser. I was younger then. I think that if a situation like that occurred now, I might handle it in a completely different manner. As one matures, your values—I don't think they change, but they modify. If I just took a coaching job tomorrow and I walked out on a deck and started coaching, I probably wouldn't be nearly as successful using the approach I used to use. I'm sure I'd have to modify my approach.

Nowadays in Southern California, you're competing for a swimmer's time in so many different ways. Some of these kids are unbelievably successful academically. They have to make a sacrifice somewhere along the line. Kids' lives today are much more complicated than they used to be. And I saw the implications of that in the latter part of my career. In part, that was probably why I stopped coaching. I never said that I quit coaching; I always said I retired. I retired from coaching in 1993, and I retired from teaching in 1998. Part of the reason I did retire from coaching was that I was seeing a change in the kids' attitude. It went against my grain. You certainly don't coach—particularly at the high school level—for the monetary reward. That was part of the reason that I felt it was time to retire. Some might say that my ideals were too rigid, but they were what they were.

I don't really regret it. I mean, I go to a swimming meet, and I think, "It'd be fun to be coaching these kids—especially the ones who are highly motivated." That'd be fun. But it's not my turn. That's what Clara and I always say: "It's not our turn anymore. We've had our turn."

Epilogue

In 2013, yet another remarkable chapter unfolded in Coach's altogether remarkable aquatic career. Unexpectedly that year, the Foothill girls' water polo coach was terminated midseason. Jim Brumm, the Foothill boys' coach, decided to take responsibility for the girls' team and to finish out the season.

Girls' water polo is a middle sport. Boys' water polo is in the fall, girls' water polo is in the middle, and swimming is in the spring. But all the programs overlap. Boys' water polo overlaps girls' water polo. More importantly, in the spring, girls' water polo overlaps the beginning of swim season.

Coach and Clara are great friends with the Brumms.

> Jim's wife, Becky, was by one day, and she said, "You know, Jim's coaching the girls' water polo team, and he's going to need some help. Would you ever be interested in running some workouts for the boys during the last three weeks of girls' water polo?"
>
> And I said that it sounded like fun. It was my intent to just help Jim through that transition. But then he invited me to stay on for the season. I choose to do that, and I got hooked on coaching all over again.

Steve Pickell was coaching the Foothill girls' swim team when Coach began coaching the girls' water polo team. Steve had a college-age son who was highly involved with lacrosse, and Steve wanted to go to some of his games. He asked Coach to run the girls' swim workouts in his absence. Coach happily complied.

In addition to coaching at Foothill and running a successful insurance business, Steve is also the head coach of the SoCal Aquatics Club—a busy man. At the end of the 2014 swim season, Steve was recruited by Tustin High to take over the swim program there. It was a difficult decision to leave Foothill, but the Tustin pool is the facility where SoCal trains. Running two programs at one pool created necessary efficiencies in Steve's busy life. He took the job, and Coach was offered the opportunity to coach the Foothill girls' swim team—pretty impressive for a man nearing eighty years of age.

> As I've returned to coaching after a long time away from it, I've enjoyed catching up on what's going on through the eyes of the coach. It's one thing to pick up a newspaper and to read meet results. Having the opportunity to be back and to actually have a hand in what's going on with the evolution of the sport—that's been really fun for me.
>
> Because of my age now, my perspective is different. It's fair to say that I see my girls now through the eyes of a grandfather. These girls are around the same age as my oldest granddaughter. So, today, I feel like I am more of a father/grandfather figure than I was—especially way back—when I was first coaching the girls' program.

The sport has changed significantly since 1993 when Coach retired the first time. These days, there is a much greater delineation between swimmers and water polo players. Workout strategies are very different. The importance of swimmers training year-round with their private swim clubs has been elevated. And advances in interpersonal technologies are also having an impact.

Orange County has become the national epicenter for water polo. When Coach retired in the early 1990s, girls' water polo teams were just getting started at high schools—including Foothill. Most of the boys' swim team played water polo in the fall and then swam competitively for Foothill in the spring. Swimming was *the* sport. Now, for many kids interested in aquatics, water polo is the focus, and there are many interesting reasons for the change.

> Having stepped away from coaching for a while and just being an observer for twenty years—wow, what a difference. The girls started playing water polo I think in 1992—the year I first retired from coaching. They quickly became the powerhouse of Orange County. I believe the Foothill girls won four straight CIF championships. They've won eleven straight league championships. They're just amazing.
>
> I used to think, "Why don't we run swim season first, then water polo?" You learn to swim and then you learn to play water polo. Or you work and then you play. The work and play thing is a real factor, I think. Would you rather work—look at a lane line on the bottom of the pool—back and forth, back and forth, or would you rather play a game? We have water polo clubs in Orange County where kids start playing water polo at seven and eight years old. They just love the sport. It's like volleyball or soccer—a team sport that they love.
>
> Water polo is the new king. And that's been a little hard for me. If I'm looking at swimming through the eyes of a swim coach, then my view is different from the water polo players who are swimming for me. They've been told forever that the better swimmers they are, the better water polo players they will be. So, many of the kids view swimming as something just instrumental—something to enhance their water polo. They're not totally involved in becoming a better swimmer for the sake of becoming a better swimmer. Swimming is a means to an end—which is water polo.
>
> For parents, too, water polo has advantages over swimming. When you watch a water polo game, it lasts an hour or so. If a kid's involved with club swimming, then a parent will go to a Saturday meet, and it can last from eight in the morning until five at night. Think about that—especially as ramped up as careers and two-parent working households are. One hour versus seven hours. And even some of the coaches feel the same way. They love swimming, but high school dual meets will start at three and end at six thirty. Other than maybe track, there isn't another sport in high school that runs so long.
>
> Now don't get me wrong, the water polo kids spend a lot of time training. There's a big commitment in the weight room, for example. But the meet itself is so much shorter than a swimming meet. I know most people don't actively look at sports from the time commitment involved, but it has to be a factor, I'm quite sure. Everyone's lives—kids and parents—have accelerated so much in the last twenty years.

Another change in competitive swimming in the twenty-first century comes from the elevated importance of club swimming.

> My experience now is that club swimming has again become so much more important than the high school program. I don't really work with the club swimmers who swim on the Foothill team. They swim with their clubs and swim only with the high school at the high school meets. High school coaches are not really very much involved with their training. That's very different from how it once was.

Splish Splash

Workouts are also very different these days. Coach remembers coaching under Lee Arth when he began his coaching career. Coach Arth was an outlier compared to how most coaches ran workouts in those days.

> Lee always said, "It's not the yards, it's the hard yards." But when I first started at Foothill, I went to all the clinics and listened to all the big-time swim coaches. Everyone hung on their every word; whatever they were preaching, that was the gospel. That's what we did.
>
> I just told the kids the other day: in those days, we would often start a workout and go ten three hundreds or ten four hundreds. They looked at me as if I'd stepped off a spaceship!
>
> Now we'll do a two hundred at a challenging time interval. We'll go a two hundred on two minutes forty seconds or two minutes forty-five seconds. We'll go into a really short rest interval. And then we'll do another two hundred. Next, we'll do a two-minute break, but during that break, we swim—one hundred yards of active recovery. The kids aren't hanging on the wall when they're resting. They're doing what we call a recovery swim.
>
> Now, when you get done with a set, you haven't gone that many yards, but you've done some incredible time intervals. You have to swim very fast to even make the interval. I always jokingly say that the faster you swim these, the more rest you get!

This practice is called interval training. The concept is that the better conditioned the swimmer is, the faster he or she recovers. The pattern is effort, recovery, effort, recovery. As the swimmer's conditioning level increases, his or her recovery time decreases. As this happens, the swimmer is able to train at a higher level of intensity.

> We go far fewer yards now than we used to. That's across the board, all the way up to the college level. Even at the Olympic level, they're not grinding out the tens of thousands of yards they used to.
>
> I've yet to do a two-hour workout this season. I write my workout, and I'll set a goal of five thousand yards. Five thousand yards is the max I give my high schools girls; the boys are going fifty eight hundred to six thousand yards in a workout. Well, we used to go to eight thousand yards—that was a short workout. And we'd work out two and a half hours. It took us that amount of time to get that yardage done. But we're now getting better results with fewer yards and less time spent in the pool.

Beyond changes in training practices, other technological improvements have influenced aquatic sports since the mid-1960s when Coach began at Foothill. Everyone who has watched a recent Olympics has noticed changes in the suits swimmers wear. In the 1960s, swimmers did not wear goggles, nor did many male swimmers wear caps. There was no digital video technology to easily capture and show swimmers video of themselves to help them improve their technique. Even swimming pools were far different then from what they are now. Competitive pools are now carefully engineered to control waves and adverse water dynamics below the surface of the water. Suits have become much more aerodynamic, and pools have become just plain faster.

Advances in personal digital technology have also affected the sport. Times from swimmers competing halfway round the world are now instantly available to anyone who has an interest in them.

Card games to pass the time at long swim meets have been replaced by all the incredible gaming, reading, and video options now available on smartphones and tablets. Waterproof digital players allow swimmers to be energized by music during long swims. And texting has turned out to be a wonderful new tool for coaches.

> Now I require all my girls to text me if they're going to be late or they can't make a workout. I want everyone to either be present or accounted for. It's great. This new technology helps me know where my swimmers are—and what they're doing—far better than in the past. That's a good thing. You don't have to wonder anymore why someone isn't at workout.

While the various swimming technologies have changed significantly over Coach's career, he has remained true to his coaching philosophy.

> I've noticed this in myself—and I've seen it in coaches with whom I've worked—your coaching philosophy remains pretty constant throughout your career. Obviously, you have to modify your thinking—or become irrelevant—in reaction to new developments. But I don't think there's a lot I'm doing differently in my philosophy of coaching. We've modified our workouts, certainly. We coach a bit differently in stroke technique. And we talk about different applications of stroke. But those things have evolved.
>
> Interestingly, swimming has evolved a great deal more than track and field, for example. Our kids are swimming faster and faster. In every single event, the times now are just amazing. I do have several swimmers from forty-five years ago whose times would fit in today. But overall, it's progressed so much, particularly with my girl swimmers. A good time for the one-hundred-yard free for girls in the late sixties might have been fifty-five seconds. Last year in CIF, we had a girl go forty-seven seconds. I have a girl at Foothill, Brooke Maxim, who regularly swims fifty-two seconds, and she has a relay split of fifty-one point seven seconds.
>
> So, swimming has, for me, evolved technically, but I don't really think my philosophy has changed much. You can't change your personality. I motivate the same—my core beliefs about people are the same.
>
> Recently, I was laughing with Clara about one of my kids. I actually lied to him, if you want to know the truth. He's a fifty-nine-second butterflyer. We had an important dual meet. These days, I'm coaching the girls, but I'm still involved and interested in the boys. I want them to succeed and excel. So, I went up to this kid and told him, "You've got to swim a fifty-eight because I have a dinner bet on this swim." You know what he did? He did a fifty-six point seven-second swim! So, I'm telling Clara this story, and she says to me, "Oh Tom. That's just you. That's what you do." And she's right. I'd have done that kind of thing at any point in my coaching career. I raise the stakes—and when I am really creative, I get my kids to help me.

In 2017, Coach will turn eighty years old. He insisted to Jim Brumm when he signed on again as a Foothill swim coach in 2013 that this coaching stint would not be as long as his first one.

> I've had a good time with this return to coaching. It's been wonderful, and it's fired up my enthusiasm. But 2017 is the year I turn eighty years old, so there's just no way that I'm going to coach as long during this stint as I did before!

Not too long ago, I asked Jim Brumm, who is fifty-seven, whether he could see himself coaching like I am when he was nearing eighty. He looked at me like I was crazy, and said, "No way!" On occasion, I've been accused of having more energy than most, and maybe this coaching thing's more proof of that. My philosophy has always been that I'd rather wear out than rust out.

A great honor bestowed upon Coach was when the new Foothill swimming complex was named after him. With the scarcity of funding in education and elsewhere, there was a faction of the school board who pushed to sell the naming rights for the facility to a high-paying corporate sponsor. Generations of Foothill swimmers and parents intervened, and the pool was eventually named after Coach.

When they put the new pool in, a couple of the board members wanted to get a big chunk of money from a sponsor for naming rights for the pool. A number of the alumni got wind of this and decided to get involved—Bruce Furniss, I know, and Ethel Reynolds and Becky and Jim Brumm—they insisted that the new pool be named the Tom De Long Aquatic Center.

They maintained to the school board that the pool had already been named. Apparently, the school board had never officially accepted that name. There was a plaque at the old pool naming that facility for me. When they tore the old pool out and put in the new pool, that's when the controversy surfaced.

I'd no inkling that anything unusual was happening. Everyone kept me out of the fray. But as I understand it, there was quite a little campaigning done—letter writing, that kind of thing—on my behalf. So, when the new pool was dedicated, it turns out my supporters prevailed—and the pool was officially put in my name.

I'm very, very honored—not only for the naming but also for the fight a lot of folks made to have the new pool named after me.

Special Epilogue Note to the Reader

As Chris Wills humorously notes in the tribute section that follows, Coach is failing his retirement! It is fortunate, indeed, that this book has taken a long time to bring to publication. Without the additional time, we would not have been able to tell the stories in the epilogue. And now, in the spring of 2017, Coach has done it again!

As you have just read, Coach has been back coaching swimming at Foothill for the past four years. He has been the head girls' coach for the past two seasons and assisting with the boys' team. Well. The boys' team won the 2017 CIF championship! This achievement fits in well with the rest of the stories in this book. The victory came down to the last event, which was the four-hundred-yard freestyle relay. Foothill High School not only won the relay but also broke a twenty-eight-year-old school record set in 1989 by the FHS boys' team. That team won the CIF championship by winning the four-hundred-yard freestyle relay. The story gets even better. The 1989 team had also broken a long-standing FHS record, set back in 1975. The record stood for fourteen years.

Whew!

This book is now going to publication. But there is no telling what other amazing accomplishments remain in store for Coach Tom De Long. We know, for instance, that all the swimmers on the

2017 CIF championship team are either sophomores or juniors. And we know that Tom has agreed to be a part of the 2017–2018 Foothill coaching staff.

So, we have thought long and hard and have decided that if you want to check in on "the rest of the story," then please e-mail Coach at delong1963@aol.com. What I can guarantee is that you will have more fun chatting with Coach personally than you have had reading this book. And Coach, as always, will make time for you—and leave you better for having spent time with him.

Go, Aqua Knights. Thanks, Coach.

Coach at the dedication of the Tom De Long Aquatics Center at Foothill High School

Tributes

Ty De Long (son)

I still can't believe my mom allowed him to do it. She had been married to him for only four years, so maybe she had not yet become the mom I knew so well from my elementary years. I have no actual memory of the day, but it's the stuff of family legends, so I know the story well.

It was August 3, 1967, the day before I would finish my second revolution around the sun. Dad decided that this would be the perfect day for me to jump off the three-meter board (also known as the high dive) at the Foothill High School pool. My father was in charge of the swim program there for the summer, so I guess he had the authority to allow an almost-two-year-old child to jump off the high board.

Although the *Guinness Book of World Records* was not contacted, I've yet to meet anyone who has gone off the high dive at such an early age. Perhaps Dad wanted bragging rights that his kid was the youngest to ever jump (or perhaps fall is the correct word) from the three-meter board. Where was Child Protective Services in the 1960s? What was my mom thinking?

At any rate, as the legend goes, I climbed the ladder on my own, and at the top, lost my balance and fell backward to the concrete deck. I fell perfectly, in such a way that my extended arm cushioned my head. As I was unhurt, I was prompted to ascend the steps to the three-meter board once again. According to the legend, my mother was there. I can't believe she let this happen.

There was no accident on my second attempt. I walked out to the end of the board and jumped, falling into the arms of my father in the deep end of the pool. Although I have no memory of this event, I know that I must have loved every second. I jumped off that board hundreds of times afterward, and I remember with fondness the rush of falling through the air and landing in the cool water below.

My father encouraged me to take risks and to enjoy living with a little danger. When we camped in the summer, he always would find a huge tree in which to build a rope swing. My sister and I would lose our stomachs in the arcs of these crazy swings. One year, he took my old Easy Rider bike from the early 1970s and flipped the frame to create a six-foot-tall bike. I had to use a fence to get on it, and I had to crash every time I wanted to get off it. One Christmas, he designed and built a toy that we called the egg. It was made from two thick egg-shaped pieces of plywood with a seat in the middle. Once belted in, the rider could rock the egg until it began to roll forward. I could get that thing moving pretty fast down our cul-de-sac. These are among my fondest childhood memories.

As a teen, I wanted to be a stuntman—probably because of all the stories I had heard about Dad's shenanigans from his longtime friends. I had also seen many of his comedy diving routines, and I would always swell up a little with pride when I heard the crowd breathe in deeply as Dad pulled off one of his crazier tricks.

In my teen years, I got into some trouble a few times when I tried to outdo my Dad's crazy antics—an impossible task. I know I caused both of my parents to worry. However, in retrospect, I kind of think it was a problem that had both genetic and behavioral roots a result of both nature *and* nurture. I am simply my father's son.

As an adult, the traits of my father that I wish to emulate are different from when I was a child. Everyone I know loves my father. I'd like to continue that legacy. His love for friends; his ability to put the needs of others before his own; his love for his children, his son- and daughter-in-law, and his five grandchildren; his sense of humor; his love for my mother; his smile; his devotion to his dog; his craftsmanship; his love for all his swimmers, those from the past as well as the little ones who come to his pool every summer; his humility; his desire to help others; and a zest for life that seems to increase with each year: this is my father's legacy.

I am still befuddled that my mother allowed me to jump off that board, but I'm glad that she did. Dad knew that both risk and excitement flavor life, and although he has taught me even wiser lessons, I'll always hold that early insight close to my heart.

Kindy De Long (daughter-in-law)

Tom is a great father-in-law. We've shared many years of good conversations in front of his fire, fun holidays in Costa Mesa, and travel adventures. I'm in awe of his good-natured dedication to his grandchildren. But from time to time, when several of my friends mention that they'd like to steal him away, they are expressing their admiration of a different quality of Tom's: his hobby of woodworking and home improvement.

Tom's generosity with this hobby has benefitted our family greatly. In the first year of Ty's and my marriage, Tom presented us with a wall unit of his own design made from knotty pine. It was intended as an entertainment center, with a spot perfectly fitted for our 1990s seventeen-inch TV set. Over the last twenty years, this piece of furniture has served a different purpose with each of our moves, and it now stands in our kitchen as essential extra cabinetry. Since that first gift, Tom has willingly dug a French drain in our backyard, built a fence, installed new windows throughout our house, built a patio cover, refaced our home with river rock, put new flooring in an entryway, built two outdoor play sets, retiled a pool, crafted a loft bed with desk, and built a Murphy bed. Our kids have logged countless hours playing with a puppet theater designed by Tom as well as an incredibly detailed train table and dollhouse.

However, as any do-it-yourselfer knows only too well, home improvement projects never go entirely smoothly. My favorite "outtake" of Tom's occurred during his construction of a play set—with playhouse, sandbox, slide, and swing set—in our backyard when my son, Evan, was about two years old. In typical fashion, Tom's design was a bit "over the top" for a two-year-old. The playhouse floor was about twelve feet above the ground, and the swing had the biggest arc I've ever seen in a backyard: about twenty-five feet. The whole project was inspired by a long, thin piece of stainless steel someone had given Tom. He thought it would make a good slide, and it did. In fact, the slide was so slick, and with such a steep slope, that it launched children rather forcefully off the end. My son quickly became proficient at landing safely, but when other parents brought their toddlers to the house, I'd always ask Evan to demonstrate, just to make sure they were OK with their children tackling such intense fun.

But the slide was nothing in comparison with the swing. Tom designed, and largely built, the play set in his garage in Costa Mesa and then transported it up to our house north of Los Angeles. He installed it in the back corner of our yard, under a large, beautiful ash tree. A wood fence bordered that corner of the yard, which was perched at the top of a very steep slope dropping down to the street below. Just as Tom was finishing up the multiday installation process, he realized to his dismay that the long arc of the swing meant that it would hit right in the middle of our wood fence. It was too late to adjust the location of the play set, but Tom was not deterred. After thinking a bit, he simply cut a hinged opening in the fence, allowing the swing to pass through. When a child wanted to swing, we opened up the notch in the fence, and when the swinging was finished, we closed it.

This clever solution meant that the highest arc of the swing brought it well out beyond the fence, into the air about forty feet above the street below. Quite a thrill for a two-year-old and his friends! Fortunately, the swing was kiddy style, with a back, which made it a *tiny* bit safer. I'll never forget the looks on other mothers' faces when they encountered that swing for the first time or the surprised gasps of people walking on the sidewalk below when a toddler swung out through the fence high above their heads. I'll never forget my son and later my daughter yelling, "Higher, Mommy!" when they were already forty feet above the ground! When our children finally outgrew the kiddy seat, we installed a regular sling seat without a back, and the swing became an even a greater thrill for them. To be honest, I never could entirely relax around that swing, but I also wouldn't trade the memories of it for the world.

In a way, the swing is a symbol of Tom's relationship with our family: love, generosity, skill, improvisation, and sense of adventure. Thank you, Tom, for all the ways you've been a wonderful father-in-law and grandfather.

Anika De Long (granddaughter)

We had just moved into a new house, and my mom and I were shopping for a bed. I knew what I wanted: a high bed with a built-in desk. We finally found the perfect bed, a wooden loft bed with desk, dresser, and fort underneath, all in one piece of furniture! There was only one problem. It was extremely overpriced. My mom tried to convince me to pick out a not-so-expensive bed, but I knew I wanted *that* bed. Without telling my mom, I went to my papa and showed him a picture of my dream bed. I simply showed him a picture. I didn't *ask* him directly to build it for me. But of course, he immediately began drawing plans for my bed.

My mom told me not to get excited because Papa might not end up building it at all. I wasn't convinced. About three months later, my mom and I spent the weekend at a church camp. I had heard that Nana and Papa would be at my house when I returned home. When we pulled into the driveway, I jumped out of the car and ran inside to greet everyone. To my surprise, my dad didn't come out to give me a welcome-home hug. I asked Nana where he was, and she told me he was in his bedroom.

I began walking down the hallway toward my parents' bedroom, which forced me to walk right past my wide-open bedroom door. As I passed by, I noticed that the walls were painted a different color. Also, my makeshift cardboard dresser was gone. I turned around and entered my bedroom. As I entered, I noticed my dad in a corner with the video camera, and on the opposite wall was my bed! I had thought that *if* I got the bed, then it would be a plain wooden bed. But my grandpa had gone all out: he trimmed the entire structure in bamboo! Also, my grandma found the Hawaiian-print fabric that I desperately wanted for my comforter, and everything was more perfect than I had even imagined.

I leaped up the stairs and onto the bed, screaming *thank you* as loud as possible. Not only had they completely reorganized my stuff and filled the drawers but also repainted the walls the exact sea-foam green color I wanted.

Over the years, my papa has added things to my bed, fixing any parts that had broken during the move, and even adding bamboo crown molding to my room! My grandma has also helped by buying a chair for my corner and helping me to organize and decorate my room. I couldn't imagine a better room.

My room is the best present, but my grandfather has also done many more things for me. I like to take my friends around the house and show them my bed. I tell them, "My Papa built it. He also built the lifeguard chair by the pool, the chest in the guest room, the cabinet in the living room, and the bed in the guest room."

He's also made me laugh so many times. One of the funniest moments with him was at dinner at a restaurant about six years ago. He was cuddling my favorite baby doll and talking to her. A woman walked by our table and commented on how cute the baby was! My grandpa quickly thought of a joke. He told her, "Yes, and look what she can do!" He lifted the doll up by one leg and dangled her in the air for a moment. At first, the lady looked horrified! But she soon realized her mistake and laughed with the rest of us.

On top of all that, my papa has taught me how to swim and dive, and he's shown me many tricks for gymnastics. He has not missed a single one of my gymnastics competitions in the last three years, and he's determined not to. He has been to too many music performances to count, and he's always ready to support my brother and me. Thank you, Papa, for being such a wonderful grandfather!

Evan De Long (grandson)

My grandfather, whom I call Papa, is an incredibly outgoing person. He can strike up a conversation with almost anyone, especially if his beloved dog, Oliver, is with him. Papa claims that he knows everyone in his hometown, Costa Mesa. Whenever we drive around the city, he points random people out, and tells me their "names": "Oh! And that guy is John. He's walking with his wife, Sally, to the grocery store. They always prefer to walk. And that person is Fred. He's a great guy."

Sitting in the passenger seat of his car when this is going on, I am always sure that he really knows none of these people. One time, when we were passing a park, as usual, he said something like, "There's Jackie and her friend Ilene." Then he did something that made me worried. He stopped the car and rolled down the window as if he was going to speak to these two people. I begged him to just keep moving. I didn't want to be embarrassed when he called out to two random people.

As the car got closer to the two ladies, Papa called to them by name. Their response was "Hey, Tom!" I was flabbergasted. All this time he had been pointing out people I thought he didn't know, and then he proved to me that he definitely knew these two people. Who knows? Maybe he knew all the other people, too. Maybe Tom De Long really knows everyone in the city of Costa Mesa.

Courtnee De Long Hein (daughter)

Tom De Long is the most patient man I know. I started driving at the mere age of ten. He would let me drive home from gymnastics practice, stopping at every light post. I loved it when my friends would tell me how handsome my dad was. I have so many fond memories of my father. One of my favorite times in my life was the trips we took to Colorado every summer. We would stay at KOA campgrounds only if it had a good tree so dad could make a chair swing for my brother and me. At the time I didn't know it, but he got caught in a tree and almost didn't get down! He has touched so many lives in such a positive way. No matter where we go, he knows someone or someone has heard of him. He is a kind and gentle man. I can't remember my dad ever yelling at me. My dad is always there for me. I am so lucky and proud to say that Tom De Long is my dad.

Owen Hein (grandson)

Some of the stuff I remember about my papa is when I was little, every time I got done eating something, he would always say, "Yummy for your tummy, sugar bear!" He always says the cheesiest jokes, but we always laugh because we can't believe he would even tell a joke like that. Last year, we flew into California late at night, and we went right from the airport to my mom's friend's house, and Papa, Eli, and I toilet-papered their house. Another funny thing about my papa is he wears a visor that looks like he has hair. Papa doesn't have any hair! Some qualities I would like to have of my papa's are his friendly personality, his ability to get along with everyone, and his striking good looks! My papa is a great role model, and I love him very much.

Elijah Hein (grandson)

Papa shaves his head. He draws with me and builds a tree house and a sandbox for me. He taught me how to swim. I love to swim in his pool and go off the diving board. Last year when he was making lifeguard chairs, he gave me the extra pieces. He gives me hugs. He always makes different kinds of pancakes, like dinosaurs, and now he lets me make some because I am older. He is cool, and he is always there for me. I wish I could spend more time with him, but I can't because I live far away in Ohio.

Abigail Hein (granddaughter)

My papa is funny. He cleans Oliver in the shower and then uses a vacuum to dry him in the garage. He made a tree house for me. When I was two, he taught me how to swim. He flips pancakes and makes them however we want. He made a bear and a cub, Mickey Mouse, dinosaurs, and a dinosaur egg. Papa made me a special dollhouse and brought it to me as a surprise from California. I like to draw pictures with him. I love him a lot.

Steve Furniss (Foothill swimmer)

Given the fact that the Furniss family has shared a special relationship with Coach D since older brother, Chip's, freshman year, a Furniss brother (Chip, Steve, Bruce, Craig) continuously swam and played polo for Coach D at Foothill from 1966 (or whenever FHS first opened) through 1977. It seems that families with multiple members, such as ours, were the norm with Coach D (Hastings, Wills, Reynolds, and a host of others, to mention a few). Due to both the span and the passage of time, it is a bit difficult to come up with a single story or memory, so for me, it is easier to reflect on several memories. Thus, most of my memories stem from my senior season (class of 1971 and his first CIF-SS championship team) with Coach D, which was special for all of us.

What first comes to mind is his 1963 Super 90 Porsche (I think he still has it), which, whenever I hear one downshifting, I am immediately transported back in time to those early (six fifteen a.m.?) and often cold mornings where I often stood huddled against the wind on Seventeenth Street, waiting for him to pick me up for "dawn patrol" practice. Like clockwork, he never failed to arrive on time, and our daily five-minute commute to Foothill was special, as he deftly maneuvered the Porsche up the back way to Foothill. The one-on-one athlete-coach relationship in swimming is unique in that the coach becomes part mentor, taskmaster, and psychologist. Coach D was all that and a lot more. Due to his relatively young age at that time of his life, he was easy to relate to and always made things fun, even when one had to put in gut-busting work in the pool every day at his behest. His fun-loving nature was infectious, and his good-natured pranks were the way he and the team broke the tedium of what the sport demands of its participants. We were at an age where we could laugh at ourselves, and it seems that he was regularly releasing someone from the surge pit or stopping us from taking the flesh off one another in the showers by snapping rolled wet towels. While giving us the perfunctory scolding or punishment we deserved, he was probably laughing along inside half the time. Every day, he found a way to challenge someone beyond the depths of his or her limits and made everyone feel good about it in the process. I will never forget some of his more ingenious practice regimens, such as chase drills, where he would spot a slower swimmer leading off first in his lane a certain time advantage and then expect each who followed to catch the one in front. I can still feel the pure pain in trying to catch my prey and Coach D exhorting, "What's wrong with you? He is only a skinny little freshman!" Unfortunately in my case, "that skinny little freshman" was future Olympic gold medalist Rod Strachan, whose future abilities were already evident. Looking back on it, he challenged you to excel on some level, no matter who you were. He brought out the best in those we least expected it from.

During the Fountain Valley Invitational (hosted by Ray Bray) my freshman year, the team decided during the meet to bounce Coach D's car (I think it was the Porsche, but I'm not sure) from its parking spot and move it elsewhere so it appeared that it was stolen during the meet. Well, some other guys on other teams joined in, and before long, there were enough guys to literally pick the car up and move it, which they did for some considerable distance. As a freshman, I was more of an observer, not knowing what the consequences would be or the protocol involved with freshman participation, but it worked like a charm, as Coach D initially was fooled into thinking it was gone. However, as Coach D has a really good BS radar, he soon figured it out and located it not that far away. That started an endearing tradition of moving his car at that meet every year. That fun was probably surpassed only by his surprise team bus stop at McDonald's in the drive-through lane with an order for forty-plus burgers, shakes, and fries. Nothing reaches legendary status faster than an unexpected after-meet food stop.

Ironically, two of my memories involve the same guy, Bob "Boney" Bonebrake (who I believe was a freshman or sophomore during my senior year and who was himself a legend in his own right at FHS). The first involved Bonebrake screwing around on the bus during a return from a dual meet that took place during a school week. It was wintertime and near nightfall as we turned from Hewes to go up Dodge Avenue where the school is. Coach D called out Bonebrake and asked the bus driver to stop. Although Coach D was fairly tolerant, Bob had obviously pushed his buttons too far on this occasion. We were all a little bit scared, as we had not seen this side of him, plus we were curious as to what he had in mind, given he had stopped the bus rather suddenly just a short way from the school. Now remember, this was before the age of political correctness, and group psychology was a key part of Coach D's arsenal in terms of both control and motivation. He instructed Bonebrake to take off his warm-ups (top and bottom), leaving him with only his Speedos (I work for TYR, and we call them racers today, but in 1975, they were definitely Speedos). At that time, you would not get caught dead outside of the pool wearing a Speedo as they carried considerable social stigma, given that a pair of tight-fitting nylon briefs was not comfortable for a young high school freshman, particularly if he was new to the sport. Horrified at Bonebrake's plight, much like walking the proverbial plank, Coach D ordered him off the bus, forcing him to walk near naked the last quarter mile up Dodge, knowing full well that one would most likely encounter fellow students departing the school. Just when one could not imagine things being any worse for Boney, a police car going the opposite direction passed. With all our faces glued to the back window of the bus, we howled out loud when the police car pulled a U-turn upon seeing Bonebrake trotting up the road in the dark and pulled over to talk with him, undoubtedly about what exactly he was up to given his near-naked state with nightfall closing in. I do not recall what Bonebrake told them, but needless to say, there was no more screwing around during bus trips that season.

Bonebrake was to get revenge later that year when someone (I cannot remember who made it) constructed a hangman's noose (complete with hangman's knots and an underlying chest harness attached). The genius of this device was that it allowed one to attach the noose around one's neck and then to a crossbar, making it look like a person had hung himself or herself, but in reality, the underharness clipped on behind took all the pressure off the actual noose that went around the neck. Immediately upon discovering this device, the team saw its true potential and hatched a plan that Bonebrake (I am not sure how he was selected, but perhaps someone thought it fitting given the humiliation of his trot home up Dodge Avenue in Speedos only) would hang himself. It was worked out the day before that Boney would be found hanging on the fitness bars near the outdoor handball courts next to the pool when Coach drove up for morning practice, since he always parked near the outside gate and moved later. Someone alerted Coach D as he arrived that morning, and since it was just daybreak, the site of Boney hanging lifelessly with a noose around his neck was not only realistic but also one of those "it sounded like a good idea at the time" ideas. Needless to say, it was so realistic that no one was willing to let it go on too long, so only Coach D knows how bad his initial thoughts were.

Now, at this point, you might say this sounds a bit sick (well, not in the minds of fifteen- to eighteen-year-olds who had to find some entertainment in a sport that asked so much from them physically and mentally every day). This is where Coach D was special. He could relate to kids and always made things challenging and fun. One might get caught up with all the pranks and laughs, but he was an extraordinary motivator, getting the best from his athletes whether they were Olympians or nonscorers. For him, everyone was an integral team member, and he knew when to challenge them and when to ease up. He knew when to crack the whip as well as when to crack a joke. He made a difference in young lives during a time in the late 1960s and early 1970s when conformity and tradition were being challenged. He taught us the value in ritual and tradition. He showed us how to lean on our teammates and to be accountable. Perhaps most importantly, he taught us respect for ourselves, our abilities, and our opponents. These are all valued life lessons that we carry with us today.

I will close with what I recall as a young person (eighteen years of age) as being the seminal moment of my team experience during high school. Beneath Coach D's outgoing and fun exterior personality beat the heart of a competitor and a great meet strategist. Our senior year (class of 1971), he knew we were good, and he planted the seed early and often that we had a chance to bring this young high school its first CIF crown. Keep in mind that the class of 1971 was the first full graduating class in school history, so in essence, we and those before us helped start FHS's aquatic tradition. We worked every day with that singular goal in mind. We won every meet, starting with the CIF relays, and beat swim/polo powerhouse Corona del Mar High School in a showdown at our pool. Everything was falling into place. People on campus knew about their swim team. Our qualifying efforts at the CIF prelims were on target, just as he had doped out the meet. It simply came down to us doing what we were capable of as individuals, and more importantly, as a team. As swimming is an individual sport, his accomplishment in molding us as a team was his true genius. Kicking Bonebrake off the bus earlier in the year and making him walk home in his Speedos had a purpose, as did everything else he did that year, from the pizza party at his home to the endless hours on the deck preparing us for "our moment." As teenagers, much of why and what he did was lost on us, as we seldom understood the real purpose behind his many orchestrations: building unity in pursuit of a shared goal. As with many things in life, a first-time experience is uniquely special, and the feelings associated with such an endeavor are seldom duplicated in one's lifetime. So it was to be with the team of 1971.

Bruce Furniss (Foothill swimmer)

I touched the wall second, behind my teammate and the heat's winner, Rod Strachan, in what up until that time was the biggest race of my life, the varsity four-hundred-yard freestyle in the CIF-SS prelims at Santa Monica High School. I knew if I hung close to Rod, then I could qualify for the finals, but it would require a huge time drop. If I did, then the team would garner some much-needed points in our effort to cement our team's second straight CIF-SS team title. I had no idea what type of time drop it would be, but when I saw Coach D's shoes at the end of my lane and looked up, the smile on his face said all I needed to know. He literally catapulted my scrawny, freshman, one-hundred-forty-pound body out of the pool.

It was May 1972. During the season, our team saw the departure of two of our best swimmers. Both were locks to score plenty of points in two individual events and a relay each—enough points to assure our team its second consecutive CIF-SS swim title. They left over a silly disagreement between Coach D and their club coach in Huntington Beach. Bill and Wit wanted to forgo training with the high school team and attend only club practices, which they felt were better suited for their training needs. Many swimming on the Foothill team swam for other clubs as well and valued our experience doing both. As a matter of fact, many of us really enjoyed working with Coach D at Foothill; we trained as a team, and we had a heck of a lot of fun.

The departure of our two top swimmers put the team in a quandary and me in a dilemma. Normally, I would have swum Frosh/Soph, where I was pretty much a lock to win one, if not both, of my races. But the varsity team needed more points than it had doped out to win the meet. If we won, then we would prevent Fullerton's Sunny Hills High School from sweeping the coveted, never-before-accomplished trifecta of CIF-SS aquatic crowns in water polo, swim relays, and swim championships.

Coach D and I agonized over the decision to swim varsity for weeks. We knew if I swam varsity, then one of the events would be the two-hundred-yard individual medley, deemed to be my best event at the time. The other would be either the event I thought was the better of the two, the one-hundred-yard backstroke, or the event where I had the most potential to improve, the four-hundred-yard freestyle. Up until then, my best time in the four-hundred-yard freestyle was three minutes fifty-five seconds, which was not fast enough to make finals. Backstroke was a good event for me but not a "great" event

Splish Splash

for me. However, my entry time in the backstroke had me seeded just outside the top six. With the four-hundred-yard freestyle, we had more upside—but a lot more risk. If I swam my qualified time, then I was assured of nothing, as my seeding was buried in the ranks of entrants. My performance would require not only a time improvement but also a big time improvement.

Coach D believed in me like no coach I had ever had before. He instilled in me the confidence that I was up for the challenge. And he knew just how to push my buttons. All he had to do was tell me the team needed it and was counting on me. For that reason and the good of the team, it was decided that I would swim up to varsity for the swim championships. And if that gamble wasn't big enough, we decided my two events would be the two-hundred-yard individual medley and the four-hundred-yard freestyle. I had been training well, and we thought I would have a time drop in the four-hundred-yard freestyle. What we didn't know was by how much.

My first event in the prelims was the two-hundred-yard individual medley. I swam well but finished seventh and was quite disappointed to have let the team down. My contribution to the team's point total was zero. Knowing I gave it my best and improved my best time didn't seem to hide my disappointment by not making the finals. Coach D was thrilled with my time and pleased with my effort. He knew it was a positive sign of what was to come in my next event, and I was determined not to let the team down a second time.

As luck would have it, I drew a lane in the first of the last three seeded heats, and even better, a heat in which Rod had also drawn. He was the heat's fastest seed. As the heat's sixth seed, I was three lanes away, close enough to see him throughout the race. Our plan was simple. Rod would swim a time we all knew was good enough to qualify safely. All I had to do was stay with him. With two seeded heats to follow ours, it was important to post times that were safely in the qualifying zone, not ones on the cusp of the top six. Coach D warned us that I had already done that—and we were not going to let that happen a second time.

Well, Rod won the heat, and I finished second, a second or two later. Coach D was so jubilant! Everyone was excited because my swim had potentially given us the cushion of points to prevail in the finals over Sunny Hills. My time drop was eleven seconds—*eleven seconds*! I went three minutes forty-four seconds. As the heat ended, Coach D raced by Rod's lane to greet me. Rod had won the heat, yet Tom made me feel as if I had. We embraced, and he literally carried me back to the team area. We all knew the importance of this swim for the team, and for the moment, I felt like a rock star.

As I reflect on that swim and that day, I realize it was the beginning of a wonderful four years of swimming at FHS and a lifelong journey of friendship with Coach D. Thanks to his guidance and wisdom, my emergence on the scene as someone who had the potential to be a really good swimmer became evident that day. There were many great moments that followed in my career, some deemed even more important by others, but none would ever be as special as that one. Coach D's guidance and thoroughness in exploring all the options with our decision to swim varsity set forth a behavior of preparation to which we always adhered. He always knew the correct decision to make, even when I didn't. Coach D was always convinced things would work out as planned. He never questioned our decisions or looked back with any regret. Coach D was ever so positive and upbeat. It was contagious, and we all wanted to catch it.

Coach D never lost his faith in me as a swimmer or as a person. He tirelessly believed in me, even when I doubted myself. The painful deliberations we endured in deciding to swim varsity or which events to swim that fateful day, as well as the mild disappointment I felt after my first race, were mere bumps in the road and treated as such. Each time I listened to him, I learned, and each time I learned, I vowed not to make the same mistake again. From then on, whenever I had a moment of doubt or disappointment like I did that day after my first race, Coach D was always there to reassure me and to give it perspective.

The outcome that day would create a trust and a bond between us that still exists to this day. No one taught me more about staying positive, and no one ever inspired me more as an athlete than Coach D. And look where it took me!

Chip Furniss (Foothill swimmer)

Throughout my swimming career, I have reserved the moniker "Coach" for a select number of very important individuals who have contributed more to my life than athletic training and instruction. My coaches have contributed life learning lessons during difficult times in my life. Tom De Long, a.k.a. Coach D, is not only called Coach by me but also by my three brothers, which places him in a unique position of respect and regard for his contributions to our lives beyond high school swimming records. As a very early recipient of his coaching efforts, I sensed a certain amount of experimentation but could easily identify the strong commitment to the team and dedication that he can keep hidden behind a smile and joyous approach to life. I would say that Coach seldom shied away from larger-than-life challenges and approached them in a way that captured others to have fun along the way.

My thoughts of our interaction are most vivid in the earliest days of the Foothill swim program, when the challenges were the greatest, and Coach D had to build from a foundation without the traditions of today. These more memorable events are also early steps in Coach D's coaching career, one that has adapted to teaching life lessons to that most difficult of individuals, the high school student, who is indestructible and knows everything.

The Furniss family relocated from Seattle, Washington, to Orange County in the middle of my eighth-grade school year, which left me as an entering high school freshman with very few friends. Like all freshmen, I was uncertain of what to do and who to trust, until I met Coach. In the beginning, as I have heard Coach tell it—and I can attest—Foothill was the "new school on the hill" with several limitations, one of them was the lack of a swimming pool. This was, however, Southern California, and several families were vocal about establishing a swimming program—my father, Bill, being among the more committed Amateur Athletic Union (AAU) parents. As a freshman, we trained at the Sammy Lee Swim School in Orange, which required us to travel by school bus at the end of the school day to the pool, and if the bus driver remembered, to come back and pick us up after a two-hour practice session.

There are several memories from these early days—freezing water, see-through gold team swimsuits, some team members refusing to swim more than two hundred yards in a set, and waiting around under the small office awning in the rain for the bus to pick us up all come to mind. However, the day Chuck Bittick joined us for practice in the pool was a season high point. The presence of a USC college All American and Tokyo Olympic swimmer and water polo champion who obviously knew Coach was beyond exciting. Looking back, the fact that we had no backstroker identified for the medley relay and none of us, including myself, had any form of a backstroke flip turn, it is clear Coach had alternative instructional plans. As I remember the day's events, after a brief question-and-answer session, Chuck got into the pool with us to demonstrate the key elements of the backstroke flip turn, a more complicated maneuver then than now. When it became my turn to demonstrate what we had learned, I was so anxious to "carry my momentum into the turn" that I charged the wall at full speed. I misjudged the distance to the wall and swam directly into it, hitting my head and knocking myself out. Years later as an entering USC freshman, Chuck befriended me and offered additional turn instruction in the USC dungeon pool, and we always remembered his day with the Foothill team and Coach D. Until his death, Chuck and his wife, Barbara, were close family friends and our dedicated family insurance agents.

Despite the training challenges of that first year, I qualified for the CIF championships at Beverly Hills High School and was introduced to "shaving down" at the hands of Coach D. Stadium seating surrounds this pool, which is underneath the basketball court. The particular intimacy of this seating arrangement lends additional focus to this story. Shaving down was a relatively new concept to swimming, and in the gender-segregated 1960s, a male shaving his legs in public was not a common occurrence. The story begins as we arrived for the CIF championship finals, a nighttime event, and took our places in the stands to wait for my first event. It was at this time while sitting in the stands that Coach D chose to introduce the lesson of shaving down. He cleared a space in the stands, and with a can of Gillette shaving cream, a bowl of water from the drinking fountain, and a two-sided safety razor, proceeded to shave my legs while going over my splits for the race. Needless to say, this was the subject of much discussion, both because of my much-improved time and because of the highly visible shave down in the stands. My father, sitting two rows up, was among the most vocal. I am not sure where the shave-down concept came from, but the razor burn from the "in-the-stands" technique was brutal. Coach D initiated to Foothill High School swimming the practice of shaving down that in subsequent years has become common practice throughout CIF but is typically conducted in a more private setting.

My brothers and I each share a unique relationship to Coach D forged from our interaction with him during one of the most formative periods of our lives. His ability to treat each of us as individuals according to our needs and deliver lasting life lessons to know-it-all high school students was a great treasure to each of us and to our family. He has repeatedly demonstrated his willingness to "coach" generations of Foothill High School students. For those who are fortunate enough to listen through the noise of their teenage years, they find a coach with the highest degree of commitment to the team and a work ethic delivered with a smile and joyous approach to life that invites others to join in equal dedication to achieve beyond their expectations.

Craig Furniss (Foothill swimmer)

I learn something new almost every time I talk to Tom. This week it was: "The best helping hand is the one you find on the end of your wrist." When Tom De Long shared this insight with me, I gave him a puzzled look, so he felt compelled to tell me it was a statement about self-reliance. While I smiled because I clearly knew exactly what he meant by the statement, I was puzzled because the best helping hand I ever had was at the end of Tom's wrist. How could a man so generous, so kind, and so encouraging not see the power of his own influence on others in the many lives he has impacted? Tom then shared the story of how, when he was in the second grade, his father put him and his siblings on the merry-go-round at the Orange Show Fairgrounds in San Bernardino and then left, never to be seen again. The average man would live a life of bitterness from an experience like this, but not Tom De Long, who became one of the great encouragers of all time and second father to hundreds of high school boys and girls over many years.

It was five thirty a.m., dark, and I was barely awake. I hated cold water in the morning (and do so to this day). My body always craved more sleep after long bouts regularly until one thirty a.m. with algebra II, chemistry AP, English lit AP, Spanish III, and so on. Most days, the *only* thing that got me to workout was the fact that Tom would soon be driving down Seventeenth Street next to our house, and he would rev the motor of his vintage yellow two-seater Porsche to let us know he was there. Every school-day morning, with few exceptions, my brother Bruce and I would sprint to the corner and pile into Tom's car—you can't be late when the coach is your ride! Being younger, I was required to straddle Tom's stick shift—no small task with the mammoth book bag I would balance on my knee. Each gear shift required me to pivot my knees and the gargantuan book bag. Tom would laugh about my books and tease my brother about the pee-chee folder he was carrying. Tom always honored my academic pursuits.

I was the last of four swimming brothers. When I arrived on the scene at Foothill, expectations were extremely high for my time in the pool. I did not live up to all these athletic expectations, but my time swimming for Tom helped prepare me for both success and significance later in my life. He taught me discipline and perspective, but more importantly, he taught me, by example, how to bring energy, enthusiasm, and fun to something as dry as swimming laps in a pool. As an intense young man from a performance-oriented family, Coach Tom would balance me with a daily dose of energy, laughter, and fun that was invigorating. When a swimming performance or water polo game did not go my way, Tom was always there to show me that not only would the sun rise the next day but also that he thought no less of me, laying out the promise of tomorrow as another day of fun, laughter, and practical jokes. The accomplishment was in having done all I could to be the best I could be, not in the result. It took me a while to understand this, but with Coach Tom, it was all about relationship and character building and not just achievement. Tom was one who knew me and appreciated me for who I was and did not just think of me as the fourth Furniss boy—that is true to this day.

My relationship with Tom started out as coach—someone who had been vital to the success and development of my three older brothers and who was highly regarded by both of my parents. It grew into something entirely more meaningful. It has been forty years since I graduated from Foothill High School, but I still see Tom regularly, and Tom and Clara are at all the milestones of my family's life (which have now evolved to significant birthday celebrations, weddings, and funerals). Tom is my friend, and to this day, he is a great source of encouragement, wisdom, and inspiration in my life.

Tom knew how to bring perspective to a bunch of self-absorbed, sometimes complaining, adolescent boys. I remember a particular day of poor attitudes in the pool. Each set Tom announced was met by groans and calls for pity for our difficult lives. I could see Tom taking this in. He immediately told everyone to get out of the pool and to sit on the concrete bench on the deck by the gym. We all sat their silently hoping he was going to send us home but had a sense we were in for an attitude adjustment. Tom gave us a ten-minute lecture on how uncomplicated our lives really were and how good we had it. He finished with, "I really feel sorry for you; the most complicated decision you have today is what flavor of ice cream you are going to have tonight. Grow up, and get back in the pool—enjoy this season of your lives. We will finish the workout." That night, I picked strawberry.

Tom always spoke the truth that we desperately needed to hear. I have repeated this story countless times to my kids.

Tom understands the power of legacy and tradition and relishes it. Tom was responsible for introducing each of our three kids to the water and for getting them to swim at a very early age. While all three chose to be athletes, none chose aquatics. None of that matters to Tom. Each of my kids has fond memories of those days in his backyard pool where they learned, for the first time, to put their heads under water. Today, all three of our kids love the water and love Coach Tom. He shares life with us and them. Last year, my daughter broke down in tears when she saw Tom and Clara at her wedding. One of the best helping hands our family has ever had has truly been at the end of Coach Tom's wrist.

Marc Hansen (Foothill swimmer)

When I was pondering how to describe Coach D, only one word came to mind: "motivation." Swimming was never my favorite sport when I was young. I did it, but I always wanted to be athletic in the sense of basketball or skateboarding or soccer—like all my friends in school. I disliked swim workouts, and swim meets were never fun because I didn't have close friends on the club swim team. A day without swim practice was always a good day as far as I was concerned.

When I got to high school, I knew that I was going to have to swim, but I wasn't looking forward to it. My sister was always talking about how much fun the swim team was, but I did not believe her. I had gone to the club team workouts to get in shape for high school swimming. I remember begging my parents to make me go only four days a week because I disliked the workouts so much. My desperation was such that I would dog my classes so I would have extra homework to prevent me from going to club swim practice. When it finally came time in February to start FHS swimming, I was dreading it.

My freshman year, we had tryouts to see how fast we could swim. It came time to do the one hundred freestyle, and I remember that when I finished my swim, the smile on Coach D's face was so big that I could see it through my fogged-up goggles. He told me I had gone fifty-five seconds, which was fast for me. I got out of the pool, and Coach D ran over to me, shook my hand, and said, "Awesome job, Marc." This was during tryouts, and Coach D had plenty of swimmers who were much faster than me. I couldn't believe it. For the first time ever, I felt good about swimming.

I swam part of that year on the junior varsity team, and I can remember how much I wanted to swim on the varsity team with Coach D. I was on the deck one day midseason, and Coach D pulled me aside. He said, "Pack your bags, Marc. You are going to varsity." The smile on his face was as big—if not bigger—than mine. From that point on, I got to swim under Coach D. League finals were especially memorable for me that year. In my first race, Coach D paced me on the deck for the five hundred freestyle. I dropped fourteen seconds, which is a large drop of time—for just about anyone.

For the rest of my high school years, I was blessed with Coach D as my swimming coach. Each year, I would be counting the days until Foothill's swimming season started. Coach D's motivational support made me enjoy high school swimming to the utmost.

The varsity Aqua Knights won the boys' CIF championship in 1989. I did not progress beyond the semifinals in my events that meet, so I watched our victory from the sidelines. I can remember when we got back to the school parking lot late at night, Coach D came to my car, shook my hand with that big smile of his, and told me that I was his secret weapon. "You will go faster than you ever have before next year!" Even though I was not a key part of the team that had just won, Coach D inspired me that night to immediately start getting ready for the next year.

I remember during my junior year that my times were not progressing as I had hoped. I was working my tail off in the workouts, but my times were just not coming down. Coach D never lost confidence in me. Every time I swam, Coach D would be right there with a smile on his face. His awesome presence made me feel good about myself, even though I was not swimming that well. Even though my swimming my junior year was not that great, Coach D always made me motivated to do better.

When it came time for my senior year, everything just seemed to come together. I loved workouts, and the meets were always enjoyable. I realized that under Coach D, I had grown to love swimming. I can remember during sprints in meet warm-ups that he just would be grinning ear to ear—and this was only warm-ups. Needless to say, that made me excited and motivated to swim even faster for the meet. I would swim my five hundreds, and Coach D would be with me all the way, pacing me from the side. When I made the CIF time trial cut at the Belmont relays, I came up to Coach D to find out how I'd done. Coach D looked like he'd won the lottery! He was ecstatic—not for himself but for me, his swimmer.

I ended my senior year in swimming placing second in the CIF fifty free to someone who went on to the Pan American games. I missed the Foothill school record by less than a tenth of a second. I was the Knight of the Year and Century League Swimmer of the Year. There is no way I would have been able to achieve any of these accomplishments without Coach D. He motivated me to swim better and faster than I could have ever imagined. He is the main and only reason I was able to excel in the sport of swimming.

Coach D, you are the most influential coach I have ever had and the best coach that any high school sport could enjoy. You nurtured a swimming ability in me that probably no other coach would have even seen. You made me enjoy swimming and believe in myself. Best of all, I got to be a part of *your* swimming world, which is one of the best gifts that I could have received. Thank you for everything you did for me. You are truly an amazing person.

Mike Hastings (Foothill diver)

Tom De Long was my diving coach well before there was ever a Foothill High School swimming program. I met him on the deck of the Sammy Lee Swim School in Orange, California, when I was ten years old. I became a member of his first age-group diving team. By the time the Foothill pool was built, Tom had already coached my younger brother, Mark, and me to full required and optional diving lists. We also acted as the straight men in his clown-diving routine.

I attended Hewes Junior High School, down the block from Foothill. Since we were already working out diving with Tom all the time anyway, Mark and I just came up to Foothill after school and worked out with the Foothill varsity team.

In those days, springboard diving was a regular part of high school swimming. Halfway through dual meets, almost like intermission, swimming events would pause as the diving took place. Most teams Foothill faced in dual meets had no divers of any skill whatsoever. By the time I was a freshman, thanks to Tom's coaching, I was pretty much unbeatable at a district level, which meant a sure point win in every dual meet. This was often important against good teams. When my brother showed up at Foothill two years later, we swept first and second place in diving in almost every meet. Ten points like clockwork.

Because Tom is a legendary swim coach, a lot of people don't realize that his aquatics background is as a springboard diver, not as a swimmer. There weren't a lot of high school coaches in SoCal back in the 1970s who knew anything about springboard diving, much less how to coach it. Yet from a points perspective, having a good diver on a high school team was huge. Tom knew this, and he started a diving team before he ever got the Foothill High School coaching job.

Tom turned out to be one of the greatest strokes of luck of my childhood. From the time I was ten years old until I left for college, I spent as much time with Tom De Long as any adult on earth. Before I ever got to Foothill, Tom regularly drove my brother and me in the evening to pools around Orange County, sometimes as far away as Long Beach, for diving workouts.

Of course, Tom always had something going on. We rode in the back of his Ford van, and he loved to sabotage us by speeding up on a road in Long Beach with a stomach-wrenching drop-off. We'd stop off at Tom's house in Costa Mesa to and from practice, and Tom would show us how he could launch his son, Ty, then an infant, into the air with his feet. (Years later, my own daughter would undergo this exact same torture.) In hindsight, it seems like I spent half my childhood on a diving board looking over at Tom standing at the edge of the pool wearing mirror shades and Adidas.

I treasure these memories and my time with Foothill's other springboard divers, including some wonderful people then named Pat Shine, Tina Summerl, and Maura Webber. But I value just as much, if not more, certain other things about Tom De Long that have little to do with Foothill High School.

Tom was a perfect counterpart and addition to my own father. During practice, working at the pool during summers, Tom was always a kick in the pants! He was up on the board all the time diving with us. He had a clown-diving routine and could do the best headfirst cannonball on earth (a talent I once saw him demonstrate by drenching an obnoxious drunk guy who was heckling him during a clown-diving act).

Tom always had a joke, story, or prank; he was forever doing nutty stuff like painting a light bulb on the O of his Ford van to mock a Ford advertising campaign. Then he used this as a reason to tell people that Ford is an acronym for fix or repair daily.

During a bad smog alert, Tom once brought an empty oxygen tank to a water polo game and had Foothill players take fake hits off it during game breaks. A ceramic vase he made spilled water when you tried to pour out of it. He had a thousand ways to make things fun.

Sunset magazine has published an article about Tom's home improvement projects. He is a world-class sailor. Who wouldn't want to be like him? And always, Tom speaks of people, even the few people he doesn't much care for, in a positive and optimistic way. In terms of how to deal with and help others, the right attitude to have, how to incorporate fun into life, how to use mischief and humor to a good end, for me, Tom is the greatest example and coach of my life. I cannot express how grateful I am to have shared in his.

I have so many stories of Coach, it is hard to pick just one, but I often think of a night when the team was on a bus coming back late from a meet somewhere. Coach was up front, turned around on one of the bench seats, telling a joke. I was sitting in the back next to a good friend of mine who noticed an off-color scene on the screen of a drive-in theater the bus was passing by. Typical of my friend, he tried to rib Coach by distracting the team from the joke, yelling out stuff like "Oh my!" and "She's taking it off!" But it didn't work! The team was transfixed on the joke, and by the time Coach got done dragging out the punch line, the drive-in and possible sex scene were long gone. There are not many people who could hold the attention of a bunch of high school swimmers under these circumstances.

Thank you for everything, Tom!

Mark Hastings (Foothill diver)

We've all heard that you know you've entered the big leagues when you've been branded with one distinguishable, universally recognizable name—think Colfax, Kobe, Tiger, or Ali. Now for you Foothill swimmers and divers out there, think Coach. And for those not directly linked to Foothill aquatics, just think Tom, or think De Long. Now, everyone, think abnormal! That's right, abnormal! It shouldn't surprise you to hear; Coach D is not normal. But who here wants any part of normal? Big leaguers are not normal. Normal is not what fun-loving people gravitate to. Normal doesn't motivate. It doesn't inspire. Normal doesn't change lives. No question about it—Coach is far from normal! Thank God for that!

I was a diver—one of Coach's many athletes—and so I will write from that perspective. All the De Long athletes will agree that, when Tom coached, it was impossible for any of us to resist his seductive charisma, his sanguine personality. Coach's training was always flavored with fun, and that's the most effective variety of coaching.

Tom is an intrinsic morale builder. He has spent a large part of his life achieving ambitious team objectives. Coach achieved his success by focusing on each individual athlete and then bonding us all together with a common goal.

Personally speaking, Tom's attention always made me feel oh-so-very special. I'm pretty sure I'm not the only person tempted to believe he or she was completely special in that he or she was the only person receiving Coach's personal encouragement. But deep down, I knew—I knew Coach's genius was his ability to make everyone feel genuinely exceptional. Tom's extraordinary talent of helping others recognize their aptitude has always been his signature trait. It is amazing how Coach De Long has inspired thousands of people, and yet, he makes each of us feel unique and exclusive. That's a gift!

Some people misunderstand success. They think success is the key to happiness. Success is not the key to happiness. Happiness is the key to success. And I don't believe I've ever met anyone happier than Coach D. This is what's so great about being around Coach—his happiness is contagious.

Coach epitomizes the ripple effect. His power to motivate and inspire transcends the individual, and amazingly, impacts others he hasn't touched directly. I know this is true because my wife, Dorothy, and I have used many of the principles we learned from Coach when raising our four daughters. When you consider the importance of Coach's ripple effect, it's truly remarkable!

I never figured out all the different parts to Tom's charisma, but I have identified two important factors: his modesty, and of course, his great wife, Clara, have fortified his influence. It is impossible to pay tribute to Coach without recognizing and honoring his beautiful wife, Clara. Clara's unyielding love, and of course, her Job-like patience, has undeniably contributed to Coach's greatness.

Life has taught me that if you are blessed with a few truly inspirational teachers, then you're extremely fortunate. Coach has always been number one on my short list of important people! I will venture to guess I am not alone with this assessment.

Thank you, Coach. Thank you, Clara. May you both continue to inspire and promote for years and years to come!

I love you, Coach! I love you, Clara!

Sharon Hastings (Foothill swimmer)

Coach has had a wonderful life and a wonderful career. He remarks often that although he loves coaching championship swimmers and divers, he equally enjoys helping his less-talented athletes excel. I am one of those less-talented athletes.

It has been my great pleasure and privilege to assist Coach in writing this book. In the process—not surprisingly—I have found myself coached toward higher goals once again. This book took far longer to complete than either Coach or I anticipated. You see, during its creation, I was challenged with a difficult, all-encompassing life crisis. Last year, my brothers Mike and Mark Hastings encouraged me to take up the work again. Theirs was good advice. Not only is this book now complete but also its completion helped me remember the useful lessons of discipline, focus, and perseverance I learned so long ago in Coach's Foothill pool. Those lessons have propelled me into a wonderful new life. Not only am I grateful to my brothers but also to Coach. Who knew that a man who factored so importantly into my high school life would now—again—coach me into success in my sixties?

In my mind, this book has worth for several reasons. First, I believe it tells the life of a great coach. I have loved learning the stories of Coach's boyhood and those of his personal athletic career. Clearly, Coach wove the hard, but mostly loving, years of his childhood into his practices of both coaching and teaching. Out of that synthesis emerged a coaching style that created a high school aquatic dynasty—and scores of Foothill athletes renowned or not—who have lived better lives because of their interactions with Coach.

I think, as well, this book helps document a certain time and place in Southern California history. Many of us who lived those years in that place feel that we were blessed to do so. Coach's time at Foothill began in the mid-1960s, extended to the early 1990s, and then resumed again in 2013. The cadre of coaches who have worked over such a span of years must be rare indeed. It's fun to read Coach's accounts of the events, kids, parents, adventures, and pranks of his long career. I suspect that some of you, reading them, may perhaps shake your heads and chuckle knowing that many of those experiences are impossible to duplicate today.

Perhaps most importantly, I think this book describes a good man. Tom De Long is a humble man, dedicated to teaching and service, who loves life and loves people. Coach attracts good people—his energy creates more good energy. Spiritual traditions encourage individuals to seek out good companions. Coach is that. He challenges, he makes the struggle fun, and he models a good and balanced life. Coach is not perfect, but he is always growing and learning.

Finally, I want to acknowledge Clara De Long. As Coach and I worked on this book, I saw firsthand how Clara is the one who has always "anchored" his story—and she kept the both of us on track to tell the important stories well. She recognizes that Coach seeks out challenges in which he has talent—and then he goes all out to achieve excellence (which isn't always about "winning"). He values "team," and he builds it always. Clara's giggles and story additions always underlined the fun and joy that are the hallmarks of Coach Tom De Long.

Thank you, Coach, Clara, and my brothers Mike and Mark Hastings—all of you made this book possible.

Chris Wills, MD (Foothill swimmer and water polo player)

Coach is one of those mentors who becomes an inspiring friend. If you look at the influence he had on all of us, and how successful "his kids" became, then it is clear how inspiring he really was. There is no doubt in my mind that he was just as much a kid as we were (although he did have a little bit more common sense than we did at the time). As we got older, we began to realize that he was just a little bit bigger kid. Today, our ages don't seem that much different. The funny thing is that, as the rest of us age, he doesn't—and he is still just a slightly older-looking kid.

Coach had a clever way of getting you to do things because you thought you wanted to. You never thought that it was what he wanted—you thought you were doing what you wanted, and he was merely rooting you on. Even though we thought we were each "doing our own thing," we somehow ended up accomplishing the things that he wanted us to accomplish. And we did it in a big way—because we all "knew" it was our own idea.

The success that this achieved was undeniable. The winning record that occurred during his coaching tenure was unmatched before or after (of course, there is no after, since he failed at retirement and is still coaching). Coach taught by example, and his energy, enthusiasm, and humor made all "his kids" better people—as well as achieving athletes. There is no doubt that his ethics, principles, humor, and enjoyment of life rubbed off on all of us. Not one of us to this day can have a discussion with fellow teammates without mentioning some anecdote about Coach that remains burned in our memories.

We are truly better people for having had the great fortune of getting to grow up under his seemingly invisible guidance.

John Seccor (Foothill swimmer)

Thinking back over the years, I often find myself pondering the many days spent around the Foothill pool. One of the things that I recall, with a bit of fascination and wonder, is just how many projects were done on or around that pool deck. Coach D was always working on something new to improve the performance of the pool. It seemed to me like he was not just coaching but always busy working on projects at or around the FHS pool.

Perhaps my earliest memory of a pool improvement project included the replacement of lane lines. The pool itself was only about three or four years old, and the lane line floats were already badly faded and breaking apart. Without hesitation or reservation, Tom tackled the project to rebuild the lane lines and replace the floats. With some help from his team members, the work was done quickly, and the new lane lines looked and functioned great.

A new touchpad timing system was another such project. Prior to their use, it was common for swimming meets to require multiple timers at each lane (all equipped with handheld stopwatches). This traditional method of recording swimming meet performances involved many participants and a cumbersome system for handling the information. It required a huge effort of coordination and management for any competitive swimming event. So, with assistance, Tom led the effort to raise funds to purchase the newest technology for its time. This improvement made Foothill's swimming program one of the most technologically advanced facilities in the Southern California region. But above all that, the new timing system permitted Tom to refocus his attention and coaching efforts on his team.

The largest project that I can recall occurred over the summer break. Upon returning to school in the autumn, we found a newly built structure on the pool deck. It was as if the "pool elves" had come and done some magic there at the pool (although I rather suspect that some of the swimmers assisted in its construction). This office, storage shed, and refuge from the weather was yet another of Coach Tom's creations. As I recall, the project was very well built and indeed served a wide variety of functions. As with other elements of the FHS pool area, Coach seemed naturally comfortable and was rightly proud of his "office" space.

Another set of activities found Coach D forever tending to and mending the pool's heater, filters, and other mechanical apparatus. I have mental images of a Charlie Chaplin character working among the gears and pulleys to make the equipment work correctly. Although I am sure my past perceptions are incorrect, it seemed as if the pool equipment always required some tinkering and attention. I do remember, very vividly, the affects that the Santa Ana winds had on the pool heater, making morning workouts a cold and uncomfortable affair. I even recall some of my fellow teammates being sent down deep into the filter tank to provide reports and/or to remove objects affecting the equipment. In the end, they all seemed to have survived the ordeal, and the pool equipment kept on running.

With so many projects going on, it was sometimes hard to see that Tom De Long was also busy with other important improvements. Even while the Coach managed these pool-related projects, he was continually working to improve the team. During both practice and competitive events, we were encouraged to do our best, chase goals, and provide our best performances. I truly believe that each athlete was given an opportunity to score points and to contribute to the team's victories.

One specific memory of just this type surrounded a CIF relay event in the early to mid-1970s. Coach had assembled an unlikely team to fill the backstroke relay event in the meet. The performance in the preliminaries surprised everyone and landed them in the finals for the event. Tom was both encouraging and loudly enthusiastic about his team's accomplishments. Although their final performance did not place first, second, or even third, they did well enough to contribute points toward a winning championship. And Coach's congratulations were every bit as earnest and genuine. A medal was awarded to this relay team but more was gained than the small token received. You see, this was where we learned something of our own individual value to a collective effort—something greater than ourselves.

Many of the Foothill aquatic athletes have gone on to do great things with their careers, their communities, and their families. It is hard not to acknowledge the hard work, fun, and sense of team acquired under Tom's leadership. We were continually being improved, strengthened, and installed as working parts of his "team" project. Perhaps this was one of Coach D's most lasting and endearing qualities. Taking these raw "materials" and putting them together into an orderly and successful assembly was a continual project. It seems now so obvious that Tom's greatest attribute was integrating a person's individual talent into the collective team effort. And we all shared in that success.

So it is with the passing of time and the benefit of perspective that I reflect warmly on these things. It was a very active time in our lives, and we shared team experiences that would later serve us as adults. For we were the team that Tom built. Thanks, Coach, for being so industrious and such a fine craftsman—just so many great projects.

David Simcox (Foothill coach)

It was in 1970 when I finished my four commitments with the US Navy and Vietnam. I had been inducted into the armed services out of college and had elected to ride out my time on a submarine during my four years of service. After I finished my commitment, I knew that I wanted to teach and coach aquatics, so I set off on my goal by earning an associate's degree at Santa Ana College and then transferring to California State University at Fullerton, where I received my bachelor of science degree in physical education and biology.

My first contact with Coach Tom De Long was during my student teaching experience at Foothill, where I had begun to realize how fortunate I was to have met this man. It did not, at that time, have anything to do with being a part of one of the best high school swimming teams in the nation. Instead, it was about the way Tom made me feel and belong at his school. He immediately introduced me to all the influential people at Foothill and even had very serious conversations with the principal at Foothill about retaining me as a teacher and water polo coach at his school. Well, it worked out, and I found myself coaching water polo at what I feel was the best school in Orange County both academically and in aquatics. Tom took extra time to show me the ropes during my first water polo season at Foothill, but it wasn't until swimming season started that I began to realize what a great person and coach Tom De Long really was.

I could talk forever about the great swimmers and water polo players who have gone through Foothill's aquatics program. Tom and I were fortunate to have been involved with very talented kids and their parents. But soon, I found myself realizing the magic formula that motivated those kids to become the best swimmer or water polo player they could become.

I watched Tom work with the swimmers and encourage them to push themselves beyond what they thought they could achieve. Tom always said, "The sport of swimming is a sport in which you can take a person of average talent, and with a good work ethic and motivation, he or she can become a better-than-average swimmer." He was like a father to them, and eventually, in his later years, like a grandfather. After a few years, I found myself counseling the water polo players and swimmers exactly like Tom would. I would watch Tom talk to his swimmers, and I could almost predict what he would say to them. I wanted to be successful like him, so I would steal every secret he had used to be successful. Things were good at Foothill aquatics.

After many years of me being the water polo coach with Tom as my assistant and Tom being the swimming coach with me as his assistant, I found myself wanting to coach more swimming. Water polo was my life, but I really enjoyed the aspect of swimmers achieving their goals by working hard at them. During my time at Foothill, I couldn't tell you how many times I saw young men and women swim incredible swims in order to win a dual meet, league meet, or CIF swimming championship. Early on in our careers, Tom and I had decided that when it was water polo season, the kids would play water polo; when it was swim season, the kids would swim. We would not ask the kids to become distracted because of another activity. The academic and aquatic goals were too high to ask kids to take on any more responsibilities. This might seem a little idealistic, but it worked for us. I would even speculate that our arrangement was probably unique in the areas of water polo and swimming. I always liked to tell the story of the 1989 swim season where six boys, all but a couple of whom emphasized the sport of water polo and one or two of them were primarily swimmers, defeated the defending CIF swimming champion, Mission Viejo Nadadores, to win the division one CIF title. Another technique that seemed to work for Tom was that, no matter how good of a swimmer you were, you would always swim the Foothill swim workouts. This was also quite unique in the world of swimming and sometimes caused a problem between the club coaches and the Foothill coaches.

In the late 1990s, Tom and I had agreed that maybe we would bring in a third Foothill aquatics coach. We were very fortunate when Jim Brumm accepted the coaching position. He had assisted Tom and me in swimming and water polo for many years until Tom retired. After Tom's retirement, Jim took over the water polo program, and I assumed the position of head swimming coach. I retired ten years later, and Jim is currently the head water polo and swim coach at Foothill High School.

As I reflect back on the years that I was fortunate enough to spend with Tom De Long, I can only consider myself one of the luckiest guys in the aquatics community. I was able to spend thirty-four years of my life doing what I loved because of him. He brought me into his world of success and enabled me to experience many of the great moments that he allowed all of us to have. Tom De Long can only look back on his career with pride because of what he created. He left a legacy of pride, tradition, work ethic, and many, many swimming championships.

Thanks, Tom. Go, Aqua Knights.

Frances H. Minnett (Foothill high school secretary)

I was the principal's secretary at Foothill High School when Tom joined the faculty. We have maintained our association throughout the years due to his teaching swimming at his home. He has taught four of my grandchildren and is now teaching two of my great-grands.

I met Tom and Clara at a Foothill High mixer in a park. Their son, Ty, was a newborn in his carriage. We all know that Tom was an excellent teacher and role model for his students. I knew him as the faculty philosopher. He knew when and when not to be the fun-loving person he was. He was a terrific jokester. It takes a really fine person to be a jokester and to still maintain the love and respect of his associates. A hectic day with sagging spirits would be brightened by Tom. Tom somehow read your feelings and knew how to lift them.

Tom had so many stories and loved telling them, as only he could. He taught so many to truly love life. I remember some of his stories to this day—and laugh.

Fred Simpson (friend)

Tom and I met in 1954 at Long Beach Poly High School. I was on the usual combination of swimming and water polo teams. Tom was on the totally unusual combination of football offensive lineman and diving teams. I couldn't believe that a beefcake like that could be so graceful on a diving board. He and Chuck Bittick also put on a great clown-diving routine. Tom had a terrific belly flop.

While we were going to college and afterward, we spent the summers working for the Long Beach Lifeguards. We had a ton of fun both on and off the beach during those summers. The pranks among the lifeguards were unending. Tom earned his varsity "prank letter" in his first summer. This, of course, set him up as a prime target.

We lived the life of *Happy Days*. We are still pals, and we're still involved in the Long Beach Lifeguards Alumni Association.

Don Covey (friend)

A brother like no other brother—you are the brother (even though I had five birth brothers) I never had in my life. How does one summarize more than five decades of our life's journeys as more than "just friends"? The good and bad storms of life that bring two kindred spirits like you and me together? Our brotherhood has always been a covenant of trust and loyalty. We knew that during life's troubled times, all we had to do was to call and know that the other would always be there—and not just be there but also giving sound advice on how to confront troubled rivers and how to rejoice in the times of small and large victories.

Tom, having you in my life and family's life has had profound and lasting effects of great influence and many memories of days gone by. I remember our first meeting in 1964 when Marge and I first went to visit you and Clara in your Costa Mesa, California, home. And the many fond memories spanning more than fifty years, such as of our camping trips, motor home trips, *Godfather* parties, sporting events, movies, our child Gents to Europe, singing "Blueberry Hills," trying to party several nights in a row, trips to Hawaii, time-share vacations, auto breakdowns in Kayanta, going to the family farms in Colorado, running out of gas so as to get cheaper gas across the street, eating more food than allowed and not admitting until many years later you took more than your share, being at our children's weddings and the births of our grandchildren, hundreds of thousands of discussions, and your stories and jokes. And being there when Marge died and welcoming Mikii into your lives years later.

Most of all—being a man of God, your modeling as a great partner and spouse to Clara, a role-model parent, a teacher, an outstanding and award-winning swimming athlete and coach, your ability to stay calm and collected while seldom losing your composure in highly stressful times, your creative ability to build with your mind and hands to make a better place for your family and friends, giving of yourself and your property to others without ever asking for a return, and just being you.

Tom, your lifetime brotherly success has always been your hallmark of courage and confidence to begin. It's the passion and persistence to continue. It's your talent and tenacity to finish what you start. It's the many roads you have traveled, the meetings of many people, the mountains you have moved, and the examples you have set for yourself and others. It's all these things and more that comprise the many successes you have achieved. And in the end, we don't just celebrate what all you have done but also who you are—and most of all, I am so proud to call you my brother.

May the love, peace, and joy of Jesus Christ always be with you.

Your brother, Don Covey

Index

Aaron, Jeff 58
Allen , Chester 39
Alter, Hobie 104
Anderson, Ron 58
Andrews, Henry 36
Andrews, Dee 36
Arth, Lee 64, 70, 83, 125
Askhy, Kelly, 66
Askhy, Shannon 66
Bainbridge, Brett 109
Bannon, Bob 58
Barnett, Bill 56
Bieney, Lauren 66
Billingsley, Hobey 47
Bittick, Chuck 38, 58, 112
Blanding, Mr. & Mrs. 2
Bonebreak, Bob 63, 89
Bray, Raymond 107
Brumm, Jim 85, 90, 123, 126, 127
Brumm, Becky 123, 127
Canham, Bill 58
Coffee, Tina 66
Courtney, Tom 58
Covey, Don 150
Cox, Jamie 66
Cox, Laurie 66
Cruz, Joseph "Bud" 1, 8, 10, 14, 16, 20, 21, 23
Cruz, Jimmy 5, 9, 10, 17, 20
Cruz, Henry 5, 9, 10, 17, 20
Cruz, Jerry 5, 9, 10, 17, 20
Cummins, Kathy 66
Lee, Great Grandpa 14
Lee, Jewel 14
Lee, Ruby 14
Lee, Opal 14
Lee, Dessie 14
Cruz, May 12, 79
Cure, Doc 36
Daland, Peter 61, 63
Darda, Jerry 78, 96
Darnell, Faye 78, 94, 96

Darnell, Floyd 45
Darnell-Merhoff, Norma 44
Dean, Lou 61
De Long, Anika 97, 99, 102, 103, 104, 117, 131
De Long, Clara vii, viii, 10, 18, 19, 43, 46, 58, 69, 70, 93, 94, 96, 97, 101, 102, 104, 105, 108, 113, 116, 117, 118, 122, 126
De Long, Joseph 1, 3, 6, 7, 8
De Long, Madeleine 8
De Long, Patsy 8
De Long, Paul 1, 2, 3, 10, 11, 17, 20, 26, 114
De Long, Paul Jr. 8
De Long, Ty 4, 64, 93, 94, 95, 98, 99, 102, 103, 116, 129
De Long, Courtnee 4, 64, 93, 94, 95, 97, 99, 100, 104, 116, 132
De Long, Norma Jean Courtnee 7
De Long, Kindy 97, 98, 99, 102, 103, 130
De Long, Evan 99, 1`02, 103, 117, 132
De Long-Hoban, Marjorie 1, 2, 3, 4, 8, 10, 11, 17, 26, 44, 45, 106, 114
Douglass, Gabby 98
Doyle, Ed 86
Drucker, Dana 66, 72
Drucker, Leslie 72
Drummund Tom 58
Easterbrook, Frank 112, 113
Ellison, Laura 66
Felder, June 85
Flynn, Mickey 37
Fullerton, Jack viii
Furniss, Bill 56, 67, 68, 92
Furniss, Chip 58, 63, 67, 68, 92, 138
Furniss, Bruce 63, 67, 68, 76, 90, 92, 127, 136
Furniss, Steve 67, 68, 76, 92, 133
Furniss, Craig 67, 68, 92, 139
Furniss, Pat 67, 92
Fury, Jack 32
Gaughran, Bob 84
Gilbert, Grandma Pearl 4, 5, 6, 10, 14, 15, 16, 17, 18, 19, 20, 21, 24

Goddell, Bud viii
Haig, Woody 58
Hall, Ted 58
Hallowell, Len 58
Hand, Don 56
Hansen, Marc 88, 141
Hartman, Jim 40
Hastings, Mark 42, 48, 53, 70, 71, 144
Hastings, Mike 48, 70, 71, 91, 142
Hastings, Sharon 70, 145, 151
Hastings, Laura 70
Hastings, Myrt 71
Hastings, Billie 71
Hauser, John 109
Hein, Abi 97, 104, 105, 116, 133
Hein, Connie 101
Hein, Frank 101
Hein, Kevin 99, 100
Hein, Owen 104, 116, 133
Hein, Eli 104, 116, 133
Hoban, Ed 8
Hoban, Jann 8
Hoban, Randi 8
Hummell, Hank 84
Humphrey, Glenn 28
Ilo, Tony 58
Irwin, Al viii, 38
Jenkins, Roger 109
Jones, Amanda 93
Kelly, Shirley 48
Kelso, Jack 43
Koval, Linda 66
Kossi, Eric 47
Lang, Stephan 58
LaRose, Rick 64, 91
Latrelle, Gary 40, 61
Lee, Dr. Sammy 31, 32, 78
Lenz, John 58
Leo, Steve 109
Levy, Dave 36
Lindley, Ted 109
Lockwood, Chuck 58
Logan, Meghan 61, 66

Lombardi, Vince 120
Lowery, Dana 66
Marcoux, Sidnainn 66
Maroney, McKayla 99
Maxim, Brooke 126
Mazurka, Deidre 66
McCormick, Pat 6, 31, 78
McCormick, Glenn 31
McCracken, Dwight 85
McIver, Jill 66
Merhoff, Paul 44
Merhoff, Kurt 44
Minnich, Frances 149
Morey, Ray 36
Mullikin, Rufus 5, 6, 10, 12, 14, 16, 19, 21, 28, 114
Mullikin, Evelyn "Peggy" 1, 3, 4, 5, 6, 10, 11, 13,
    14, 16, 17, 18, 19, 20, 22, 23, 28, 40, 44, 68, 114
Murphy, Tom 38, 40, 41
Nabor, John 76
Neimi, Emil 94
Newland, Ted 55
Nitzkowski, Monte 32
Olszewski, Johnny 49
Osborne, Bob viii, 55
Painter, Mr. 20, 21, 25
Palchikoff, Jay 63, 70
Palchikoff, Jan 70
Palchikoff, Kim 70
Palchikoff, Kai 70
Palchikoff, Nick 70
Palchikoff, Dawn 70
Peck, Dick 31
Pfremmer, Dale 101, 103
Pfremmer, Cloyes 101, 103
Pickell, Steve 123
Piers, Kathleen 66
Prigmore, Dan 58
Ray, Scrappy 49
Reece, Tracy 66
Reece, Rhonda 66
Reynolds, Laura 66, 69
Reynolds, Ed 69
Reynolds, Julie 66, 69

Reynolds, John 69
Reynolds, Kathy 69
Reynolds, Mike 69
Reynolds, Robert 69
Reynolds, Frank 69
Reynolds, Ethel 69,127
Richards, Bob 74
Richardson, Dean 39
Rogers, Wally 31, 32
Runnels, Dr. Charles 98
Sadaro, Dave 71
Salata, Steven 72, 92
Salata, Jason 72, 92
Schuessler, Adian
Seccor, John 146
Sedoo, Jerry 55, 57»
Shafer, Wayne 109
Shipp, Matthew 36
Shsorsky, Don 47
Siegel, Bugsy 12
Simcox, David 69, 84, 85, 90
Simcox, Kathy 69
Simpson, Fred 50, 115, 149
Smith, Jim 36
Smith, Dick 42, 78
Snyder, Bill 85
Spitz, Mark 76
Spurzum, Peter 108

Strachan, Rod 76, 77
Strenk, Andy 83
Summerl, Dale 58, 72
Summerl, Dan 58, 71
Summerl, Tina 63, 66,71
Summerl, Dick 71
Summerl, Lois 71
Teeter, Ralph 57
Timberlake, George 49
Underwood, Bill 47
Urbanchek, John 83
Wagner, Taylor 81
Ward,G.B. 80, 81
Webster, Bob 32, 95
Whitinaw, Richard 58
Wills, Chris 68,107,127,146
Wills, Kenny 68
Wills, Bob 68
Wills, Maralys 68
Wills, Tracy 69
Wills, Eric 69
Wills, Bobby 69
Wilson, Pat 43
Wiseman, Claude 57
Whitaker, Susie 70
Wooden, Johnny 73, 120
Wrightson, Bernie 41, 42, 53

Author Biography

Tom De Long spent more than fifty years as a coach and mentor to countless swimmers, divers, and water polo players in Southern California.

Sharon Hastings lives in Ephrata, Washington. A former Foothill High School swimmer, she is grateful for the opportunity to preserve De Long's legacy.

Appendix A

Letter to the First Foothill Swim Team, 1966

Welcome to the first swimming team at Foothill High School. The challenge will be great, but the rewards will be much greater. 1966 will be a year for setting traditions for every swimmer who follows this first team.

We will start next Monday in the pool. Each boy who comes out will be timed for fifty yards freestyle and fifty yards of any stroke he chooses. Our workouts will be very hard, and the boys who stick it out will reap the fruits of hard work. Our goal from the very start will be to place Foothill on the Southern California swimming map. I know Foothill is going to become an outstanding power, and I welcome each of you who want to become a part of it.

Those of you who stay will know what it is to sacrifice. If you are to become an asset and a successful member of Foothill's swimming team, and if you expect to develop into the best swimmer that your natural ability and physical build will permit, then consider well the following:

a. Decide definitely that nothing, barring illness or injury, will keep you from becoming outstanding in this sport.
b. You must, during the season, consider this sport as next to your scholastic and family responsibilities in importance.
c. Headwork (brains) must be used during all practice periods. It is important to be mentally alert during every minute of your practice period. Analyze every stroke, every turn, and every start during practice.
d. You must get wildly enthusiastic over water events, and you should seek every opportunity to be in or around swimming events.
e. Consider carefully the following: live right, think right; seek wholesome companions; get your full quota of sleep; do little or no eating between meals; shun smoking; shun drinking; select your girlfriends among those who will inspire you to follow our training rules; and most of all, cooperate with your parents, as they are your greatest boosters.
f. Repeat to yourself each day: what I am to be, I am now becoming.

Our program is a stiff assignment. It will take a boy with real "stuff" to carry it out. A weakling will not even try to tackle it. This is your coach's challenge to you.

T. E. De Long, Foothill Swimming Coach

Appendix B

Diving Dictionary: To Coach with Love 1977

By Mogul (Mary), Bear (Tina), Birdseed (Linda),
Jet (Heidi), Butch (Laurel), and Frito (Leann)

A
A body in motion tends to stay in motion. Will no doubt go down in American history, along with baseball, hot dogs, apple pie, and Chevrolet.
Are you in love? A subtle hint that our minds aren't on diving.

B
Back slappers. Usually demonstrated by Bear, who has the bruises to prove it. Precautionary measure: wear FHS athletic department wash-and-wear sweats.

C
Chest up. No comment.
Chort. Been cruzin' in S. A. Valley's neck of the woods lately, Coach?
Con sis tent\-+ ent\ (adj). 1. Uniformity; 2. To be inherent; 3. One of our required vocabulary words.

D
Did I ever tell you the one about the… Time for one of Coach's forgettable jokes.
Diver's relay. When divers get together and organize a swim relay five minutes before the event—and end up winning.
DPH. Dives per hour. Usually decreases to ten DPH when it's cold or after someone smacks.

F
Face-ripping tool. Coach's new invention to be used on divers who don't do as they are told. Patent pending.

G
GFI. Go for it.
Go kick the football. Lead-up dive. Does this give you the idea that Coach would rather be in a different sport?
Go on up. No, not to Thurlow's office but to the three-meter board. Personally, we'd sometimes rather go on up to Thurlow's.

H
Hut-hut. More football overtones.

Tom De Long with Sharon Hastings

I
I'd tell you if you were going to hit the board. Sure, Coach. It's just your timing that we aren't sure of.

L
Let the board lift you. But we're so anxious to hit that nice warm water.
Looks like you're wearing your mother's army boots. Your toes aren't pointed.
Lorene special. Cannonball.

O
Official diving ditty.
    I love my wienie man.
    He loves his hot dog stand.
    He sells most anything—from hot dogs
    on down. Someday I'll be his wife
    His little wienie wife.
    Hot dog! I love my wienie man.
Oh, ah. An audience-witnessed face or back slapper.

R
Riverside. Where most of us would like to be instead of doing this dive.
Rotate over the board. What do you think we are? Helicopters?

S
Stand up off the board. Walk on water, Coach?
Stomp. Either Bigfoot joined the team, or we are wearing our mothers' army boots again.

T
Tell 'em birdseed. You wienie!
The diving board is fixed at one end. One of the most repeated lectures—told only when we need reassurance that we won't hit the board. (Usually said every day.)

Y
You BA. You had better believe it, Chick!
You look like something that fell off a freight train going 190 MPH. Coach, in one of his more complimentary moods.
Your eyes weren't open, were they? So that must be why I couldn't see the water.
Your legs look like Jell-O. Better Jell-O than yellow, Coach.